Professional Education

PETER JARVIS

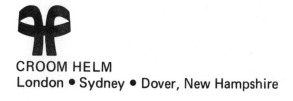

CROOM HELM
London • Sydney • Dover, New Hampshire

© 1983 P. Jarvis
Croom Helm Ltd., Provident House, Burrell Row,
Beckenham, Kent BR3 1AT
Croom Helm Australia Pty Ltd, Suite 4, 6th Floor,
64-76 Kippax Street, Surry Hills, NSW 2010, Australia
Croom Helm, 51 Washington Street,
Dover, New Hampshire 03820, USA

First paperback edition 1984
Reprinted 1986

British Library Cataloguing in Publication Data

Jarvis, P.
    Professional education. – (New patterns of
    learning series)
    1. Professional education
    I. Title II. Series
    378'.01   LC1059

    ISBN 0-7099-1409-1
    ISBN 0-7099-1456-3 Pbk

Printed and bound in Great Britain
by Billing & Sons Limited, Worcester.

PROFESSIONAL EDUCATION

NEW PATTERNS OF LEARNING SERIES
Edited by P.J. Hills, University of Leicester

An Introduction to Educational Computing
Nicholas John Rushby

Preparing Educational Materials
N.D.C. Harris

The Organisation and Management of Educational Technology
Richard N. Tucker

Adult Learning
R. Bernard Lovell

Evaluating Instructional Technology
Christopher Kay Knapper

Assessing Students, Appraising Teaching
John C. Clift and Bradford W. Imrie

Student Learning in Higher Education
John D. Wilson

Learning and Visual Communication
David Sless

Resource-based Learning for Higher and Continuing Education
John Clarke

Learning to Learn in Higher Education
Jean Wright

Education and the Nature of Knowledge
R.J. Brownhill

Learning in Groups
David Jaques

Video Production in Education and Training
Geoff Elliott

Lifelong Learning and Higher Education
Christopher K. Knapper and Arthur J. Cropley

Educational Staff Development
Alex Main

Teaching Learning and Communication
P.J. Hills

CONTENTS

To Maureen, Frazer and Kierra

without whose understanding this book would never have
been written

NEW PATTERNS OF LEARNING

THE PURPOSE OF THIS SERIES

This series of books is intended to provide introductions to
trends and areas of current thinking in education. Each book
will be of interest to all educators, trainers and administrators
responsible for the implementation of educational policies and
programmes in higher, further and continuing education.

The books contain a bibliography of key works to enable the
reader to pursue selected areas in depth should he or she so
wish.

This book, 'Professional Education', examines the changing
concept of education and looks at the aims, curricula and
methods of appraisal of professional education. The book is
written by Dr Peter Jarvis who is a Lecturer in the Department
of Adult Education at the University of Surrey.

P.J. Hills
Leicester

ACKNOWLEDGEMENTS

Many people have assisted me in writing this book - too many to
name all of them individually, although I should like to identify
some of them here.

This book was originally to have been written jointly by Miss
Pat Smart, senior lecturer in Philosophy at the University of
Surrey and myself, but due to circumstances beyond her
control she has had to withdraw from this joint enterprise.

Some of the ideas discussed here have been raised with
students on the Post Graduate Certificate of Education of Adults
course, organised at the University of Surrey. All of these
students are preparing to teach adults, mostly in the professions,
and I am grateful for some stimulating sessions that have helped
me clarify some of my thoughts.

Miss Sheila Gibson, a colleague in the Department of Adult
Education, who encouraged me to write this book, has kindly
read the manuscript and has helped me correct some of the
worst excesses of my written style. This has been an unreward-
ing undertaking for her but one which will result in the book
being easier to read.

Dr Philip Hills, the editor of this series, has been a constant
source of support and I am most grateful to him for his support
while I have completed the book.

Hilarie Morgan has typed this manuscript with considerable
skill, speed and with much patience. Without her efforts the
book would not have been produced as rapidly as it has been.

Finally, this book is dedicated to my wife and children who
have encouraged me to use spare time in the evenings and at
weekends to write and have made few demands upon me during
this period.

I am grateful to all who have assisted me in any way, but, in
the final instance, none but me can take responsibility for the
ideas expressed in the following pages.

P. Jarvis
University of Surrey

1 THE CHANGING CONCEPT OF EDUCATION:

THEORY AND PRACTICE

Education is usually associated with childhood. Stop anyone in
the street and ask them about it and invariably they will reply
in terms of schools and schooling for children. Read books on
educational theory and the majority of them will refer to the
education of children. True, much education is about bringing
up and teaching young people and even the word 'education'
may be derived from the Latin 'educare' which means 'to train
or bring up a child'; hence, the term may be being employed
correctly according to its derivation. But there is a possibility
that the word stems from another Latin word ('educere' denoting
'to draw out' and if this were the case then the traditional usage
of the word is not in accord with its derivation. It is unfortunate,
but quite understandable, that the taken-for-granted meaning
of the word refers to the first of these two derivations although
it will be argued in this book that this is a very limiting use of
the word, since logically education can occur at any stage in life.
However, it is only with more recent developments in the education of adults that the illogical use of the concept has begun
to be recognised. One of the main intentions of this book is to
begin to formulate some ideas about education, but which examine
it from the totally different perspective of the education of
people in a variety of professions. Even so, many of the ideas
discussed here might prove useful to other educators, especially
those who teach adults.

Since the concept of education has generally been assumed to
relate to childhood, it is necessary from the outset to reconsider
its meaning and this is the purpose of this opening chapter.
Having formulated a concept of education, it is intended to
explore what is actually occurring in the world of education at
the present time in order to demonstrate the realism of the
definition provided here. At the same time, it is necessary to
refer to other discussions on the subject but it would be most
tedious to employ a multitude of studies, so that most of the
references here will be to one of the most influential writers in
this sphere, R.S. Peters, whose work will be examined in some
detail.

THE CHANGING CONCEPT OF EDUCATION

Many of the earlier definitions of the term 'education' reflect
the meaning of 'educare' and include within them an intra-

1

generational perspective. John Stuart Mill, for instance, claimed
that the content of education was to be found in 'the culture
which each generation purposely gives to those who are to be
their successors' (cited in Lester-Smith 1966:9). Similarly, the
early French sociologist and educationalist, Emile Durkheim
(1956: 71) regarded education as 'the influence exercised by
adult generations on those who are not yet ready for social life'.
Yet by the beginning of this century it was becoming apparent
that an inter-generational perspective is not intrinsic to the
concept of education. For example, John Dewey (1916: 8) had to
add a prefix to the term education in order to express the same
type of idea as that specified by Mill and Durkheim, noting that
formal education was necessary if society was to transmit all its
achievements from one generation to the next. While 'formal'
would not now necessarily be the prefix employed, 'initial' might
be more meaningful, it does denote Dewey's recognition that
education is a broader concept than that of the education of
children. Indeed, he argued that education could occur at any
stage in life, so that while education and the education of
children are related they are self-evidently not synonymous.

More recently, Peters (1966: 23ff), following Wittgenstein's
argument, has claimed that education, like many complex
phenomena, is too complex to be defined. He goes on to suggest
that these complex concepts form a family 'united by a complicated network of similarities overlapping and criss-crossing;
sometimes overall similarities, sometimes similarities in detail'.
However, the question then must be posed as to whether the
whole family needs to be defined, or may not the similarities that
unite the family then constitute the basis of the definition?
Peters has sought to isolate these similarities but instead of
doing so from an empirical perspective he has attempted to
specify criteria that define what is, and what is not, an educational process. But before these can be discussed in detail it
is necessary to clarify any problems that surround the concept
of definition itself.

Traditionally, a definition is an endeavour to construct conceptual boundaries around a phenomenon, so that everything
encompassed within the boundary line may be classified as being
of that particular phenomenon and everything that lies beyond
it is excluded. Yet as phenomena have become so complex and
as one phenomenon has merged into another in the complicated
growth of industrial, urban society, it has often become
extremely difficult to isolate and delimit specific phenomena: it
is more common nowadays to question the validity of employing
definitions. Yet to employ a word without overt definition is
not to mean that the user of the word does not have a covert
and implicit definition. As this is the case, it is considered
wiser for the purposes of this discussion to attempt to provide
a meaning to the term. Nevertheless, no attempt will be made
here to demarcate the external boundaries of the phenomenon,
rather this approach fastens on to the similarities that constitutes

the family and endeavours to define education by them. This is
precisely what Peters has done in specifying three criteria of
education and he argues that these criteria constitute the basis
'to which activities or processes must conform' (1966: 25) if they
are to be regarded as educational. He is, therefore, claiming
that anything that lies beyond his criteria is not educational
and all that falls within them is educational. His criteria, therefore, perform precisely the same function as a definition,
although now the extreme limits are no longer specified. While
Peters has constructed his criteria by logical argument, it
would have been possible to have analysed the social reality and
to have extracted the highest common factors from all the
observations. However, the problem with the empirical approach
is that a covert definition/set of criteria of the phenomenon (a
working definition) must already exist in the mind of the
investigator before the inquiry is undertaken. It is, therefore,
more logical to commence with a conceptual analysis, leading to
a rational definition and then using it to examine the social
reality. If the criterion/criteria are sound, then the definition
should be realistic but if they are not then the logical process
by which they are construed requires further examination.

It would perhaps be useful at this juncture to examine Peters'
argument a little more closely. He suggests that:

'Education' is not a term like 'gardening' which picks out a
particular type of activity. Something, of course, must be
going on if education is taking place and something must have
gone through for a person to emerge as an educated man. For
education is associated with learning, not with a mysterious
maturation. But no specific activity is required . . . (1966:
24ff)

He then goes on to discuss his three criteria of education, but
before these are examined, it is necessary to question this
analogy. Education is associated with one particular activity,
that of learning and, while it may occur in numerous contexts,
it is most certainly an activity. But it is a mental activity rather
than a physical one so that it is not always observable. Yet
because it is not seen it does not always mean that it does not
exist! It is, therefore, argued here that education is always
associated with a specific activity - that of learning. But is it
not also always associated with teaching? Is not education about
a process of teaching and learning? Once more the traditional
picture of children's education emerges - the teacher, the children and the school. What of the mature adult who reads widely,
compares analyses from one study with another, reflects upon
what he reads, learns and demonstrates what he has learned by
passing examinations or writing an original piece of work? It
would be hard to deny that he had not undergone an educational
process and yet it is difficult to locate either a teacher or a
school. Hence learning, but not teaching, is the similarity that

binds the education family together. Even so, education is not
synonymous with learning, so that it would be false to define the
former in terms of the latter alone. Education is about a process
of learning, but before it can be defined, the criteria of the
educational process need to be constructed.

Education is about a learning process, so that at the outset
the word 'process' needs discussion. As a noun, process may
mean: a course of action; a series of incidents; a method; an
action at law; an outgrowth. The last of these five meanings is
specific to anatomy, zoology and botany and the penultimate one
is confined to legal actions, so that neither of these relate to
the discussion about education. The methodology of process is
itself problematic but since a chapter of this book is devoted to
methodology no further reference will be made to it here.
However, the first two meanings of the word - 'a course of
action' and 'a series of incidents' - are much more significant to
this present discussion. Education is certainly not a 'one-off'
occurrence but it is about a series of events in which learning
is intended. The idea of 'series' suggests that the incidents may
be continuous or recurrent, neither being mutually exclusive.
However, the first meaning suggests that something is actually
planned or intended. Learning is obviously intended when the
learner embarks upon the process but, it may be asked, does
the fact that some learning may occur without planning exclude
it from being classified as education? When a learner, reflecting
upon incidents which have occurred in his life which were not
intended but from which he has learned, classifies them as
educational experiences, is he actually employing the term
correctly? It might appear dangerous to exclude the possibility
of learning from ordinary, everyday experience as educational,
but not to do so may create even more problems because there
would then be no reason for excluding the whole of the socialisation process from the ambit of education. Once this option
exists education may appear synonymous with learning or it is
so broad a concept as to be virtually meaningless. It is, therefore, considered here that an element of planning is essential
to the educational process so that education may be viewed
tentatively in terms of a planned series of learning incidents.

Nevertheless, the word 'plan' does initially prove difficult.
As Hare (1964: 47ff) has suggested, indoctrination may be
viewed as an intention as well as either the content or the
methods of the process. It is, therefore, important to qualify
the idea that education is a premeditated process by excluding
such possibilities as 'indoctrination'. This may be possible by
recognising the essentially humanistic quality of education, as
Dewey (1916: 23) has emphasised:

> Knowledge is humanistic in quality not because it is about
> human products in the past, but because of what it does in
> liberating human intelligence and human sympathy.

Consequently, Dewey regards education as the antithesis of indoctrination: the one frees the mind whereas the other binds it. It is, therefore, argued here that the planned process of education must have incorporated into its definition some reference to the humanistic quality of the enterprise. By so doing, such processes as indoctrination may not be legitimately included within the conceptual framework of education.

Yet the word 'learning' still requires discussion before an operational definition of education can be formulated. Learning may be regarded as the acquisition of knowledge, skill or attitude by study, experience or teaching. Yet even here no reference is made to the level of knowledge attained nor to the degree of understanding. It would be, and is, possible to learn a mathematical formula by rote but be neither able to understand it nor apply it. It would be illogical to consider an individual who learned without understanding as having been educated. Hence education is more than merely a process of learning: it is a process of learning and understanding knowledge, skill or attitude.

Implicit within the term 'understanding' is the recognition that the learner can both evaluate the knowledge, skill and attitude learned and also reject that which is false, irrelevant or of no value to him. Discrimination lies at the heart of understanding.

It is now, therefore, possible to propose a definition of education - one that will form the basis of the discussion in the following pages.

Education is any planned series of incidents, having a humanistic basis, directed towards the participant(s)' learning and understanding.

Clearly this definition requires discussion, so that its implications are now examined and then related to Peters' three criteria.

It might be objected that it is impossible to plan for understanding to occur, but this is not so! It is not possible to guarantee the outcome of a series of events and, consequently, this definition makes no attempt to specify what the results will actually be. Yet it is maintained here that education must have aims, or else the process will not really be education. Even so, it is quite understandable for someone, reflecting upon the learning and understanding gained from an unplanned series of occurrences, to classify those experiences as educational, although they may not actually have constituted an educational process. Education should always be a planned process directed towards learning and understanding, but the individual branches of education must specify their own aims. The third chapter of this book, for instance, is devoted to a discussion of the aims of professional education.

Similarly this definition does not specify what is to be learned, or taught; the content of the curriculum is not a matter for

the definition of the process. Further reference will be made to
this below in discussing Peters' first characteristic of education.
Nevertheless, it is to be noted here that this definition is wide
enough to embrace knowledge, skills and attitudes essential to
the concept of professionalism as well as the cognitive emphasis
of higher education. Yet it is narrow enough to rule out as non-
educational those processes that do not enhance the humanity
of the participants during the process of acquiring knowledge
and understanding.

The definition does not specify, however, that education is
a process of teaching and learning since it is claimed here that
while learners are essential participants in the process, teachers
are not! Gross (1977) indicates how some lifelong learners have
planned their own learning programmes and have embarked upon
the educational process without necessarily including, or
utilising, a teacher, but it would be impossible not to consider
some of these persons as being highly educated persons. Neither
does the definition actually specify that there need be two
distinct processes: the teacher externalising and the learner
internalising. Paulo Freire (1972: 60ff) rightly recognised that
the teaching and learning process is a dialogue in which the
teachers are also learners and the learners teachers and this
conception may also be understood within this definition.

Teaching and learning have frequently been taken to imply
the inter-generational process, as included in the definitions
given in the introduction to this chapter. Clearly in professional
education there must be some idea, at least in its initial stages,
of new recruits learning about that which is already established
within the profession. However, in the other forms of post-basic
and in-service education this need not be the situation. The
elite of hierarchical professions, for instance, can go on a
continuing education course and be taught by their subordinates
within the hierarchy. In adult education, the elderly may be
taught by those younger than themselves. Education per se is
not concerned with the knowledge, skills and attitudes that one
generation wishes to transmit to the next: it is concerned with
knowledge, skills and attitudes that may be learned by people
of any age.

It will be seen from this discussion that already different
branches of the process are appearing, but before an elaboration
of the more complex phenomenon of education is embarked upon
it will be useful to re-examine Peters' (1966) three characteristics
of education.

*Education Implies the Transmission of What Is Worthwhile to
Those Who Become Committed to It*

Education has been claimed to be normative by many philosophers
and they claim that this is a better perspective than the more
value-free one that seeks merely to define the process. Frankena
(1973: 23) holds that it should be adopted because 'only then

will we have a concept of education that can guide us as a pillar
of cloud by day and a pillar of fire by night, rather than the
other way around'. However, there appears to be considerable
confusion surrounding his discussion: he argues that it is very
necessary to foster in children 'this sense of what is desirable
or relevant' (1973: 27ff) and goes on to write that he is unable
to suggest who should determine what is desirable and that
every man may be his own philosopher about what is worthwhile.
Thus a specifically normative approach to what is transmitted/
learned may be too vague to be incorporated into a concept of
education. It would also appear to be more relevant to note that
what is incorporated into the curriculum of an educational process
may be there for certain reasons, one of which may be that the
content is considered to be worthwhile. However, to claim that
the criteria, the selection of curriculum content, is necessarily
intrinsic to the educational process appears to be rather
excessive, since there are many other criteria that have never
been viewed as necessary to the concept of education.

It is acknowledged, however, that there is a sense in which
the definition of education suggested here is normative since
it is claimed that the process is of a humanistic nature. The
participants in the process must have the opportunity to realise
and develop their humanity through the process, or else it is
not education. Through learning and understanding the participants might grow and develop and in as much as human
development occurs through education then the process is 'a
priori' beneficial. Yet it must be recognised that there are
instances when the educational process may not be beneficial
to the learner, such as the trauma experienced on learning that
a highly valued belief is false knowledge.

Closer analysis of the wording of this characteristic also raises
questions about the word 'transmission' which implies but does
not specify, that a teacher is necessary to the process. Additionally, it suggests that commitment to the content is necessary by
the participants but this is to confuse motivation with the educational process and this is not necessarily intrinsic to education,
even though it is a planned process.

*Education Must Involve Knowledge and Understanding and Some
Kind of Cognitive Perspective, Which is not Inert*

Peters argues that education involves knowledge and understanding which is taken to be similar to the process of learning
and understanding that occurs in the definition formulated
above. However, Peters certainly places a greater emphasis on
the cognitive aspect than that specified in the definition adopted
here. Nevertheless, it will be argued later in this book that the
content of professional education is knowledge, skills and attitudes - but that in order for the process to be educational,
there must be a knowledge basis even to skills performance.
Indeed, it is suggested here that a person who has knowledge

without skills may be as incomplete a human being as one who
has skills without knowledge, and since ultimately the bene-
ficiaries of the educational process are people - their development
is one of the final criteria in deciding the value of education.

Peters' second point about inertia is one having two facets to
it. First, he claims, that what is learned must result in an
individual's outlook being transformed by its acquisition and,
secondly, that it implies that the learner must be 'inside' the
knowledge and committed to understanding it. These two elements
both relate to professionalism and professional practice, so that
they are important to an understanding of the process and out-
workings of professional education. Clearly there is a third
element to inertia: that of active participation in the learning
process which may facilitate the learning and understanding
being more efficient. However, some form of activity may be
intrinsic to the process of learning and understanding and implied
within these terms. Nevertheless, Peters' other two points may
occur as a result of the process's aims being successfully
achieved and, as such, may not be intrinsically related to the
actual process of education per se and for that reason further
discussion about this will be left until elsewhere in this book.

Education at Least Rules Out Some Procedures of Transmission, on the Grounds That They Lack Either Wittingness or Voluntariness on the Part of the Learner

Peters (1966: 37) writes that education 'picks out no particular
process; it implies criteria which processes must satisfy'. However, no actual criteria are specified in these three sets of
characteristics apart from the fact that the learners in the process must be active, willing and voluntary. By specifying that
education is a planned series of events of a humanistic nature
directed towards learning and understanding, there is an
implicit element of active participation in the educational process
on the part of the learner. However, the word 'voluntary' raises
problems about children who attend school because it is the legal
requirement that they do so. They may be stimulated/motivated
to learn by the teacher and they may actually become willing
and voluntary learners, so that in this instance these criteria
would apply. Nevertheless, in the first instance the learners
were involved in an educational process but they were perhaps
less than voluntary. If education may occur in one instance
without voluntariness on the part of the learners, however
desirable it may be that they do not participate in the process
out of a sense of compulsion, their voluntariness is not an
intrinsic part of the educational process.

Yet the emphasis on 'the humanistic nature' of education in
the definition posed here answers some of the points implicit in
Peters' third characteristic: it does, for instance, rule out
certain methods as being non-educational on the grounds that
they deny, or at least they do not take fully into consideration,

the humanity of the participants. However, it is preferred here
to formulate the educational process in terms of the humanity
of the participants rather than attempting to specify which human
characteristics are essential to an understanding of education.

It is suggested, therefore, that Peters' characteristics of
education are not all intrinsically connected to the educational
process as defined in this chapter. Neither may they actually
be a clear reflection of certain forms of education that occur
within the complex phenomenon which is being discussed here.
They may, however, reflect an undefined conception of education
that remains implicit in Peters' work, but since his theorising
relates much more specifically to one branch of education, initial
education, it is probable that these characteristics are more
directly relevant to a discussion of this branch of education
rather than to education per se. It is maintained here that the
definition of education offered in this chapter is applicable to
the stem from which all branches of the phenomenon have
grown, even though each will have to be qualified according to
its own especial mode of classification, so that it is now necessary
to explore these different branches of education.

BRANCHES OF EDUCATION

It was suggested in the previous section that education has a
common stem and a multitude of branches and the purpose of
this brief section is to explore some of these different branches
of education. Education, it was argued, is any planned series
of incidents, having a humanistic basis, directed towards the
participant(s)' learning and understanding. However, even in
the last section it proved impossible to discuss any of the manifestations of this process without first having to add a prefix,
e.g. continuing, moral, to the term 'education', in order to
clarify the particular manifestation to which reference was being
made. Indeed a plethora of prefixes may be discovered, all of
which endeavour to describe a particular type, or branch, of
education so that this sub-section will focus upon these different
branches. The ensuing analysis does not seek to be exhaustive,
although included within it are many terms in common usage.
   Merely to list the terms would not be of great benefit so that
an attempt has been made here to classify the types of education
into some of the main branches. However, it must be recognised
that many of these prefixes are not themselves used unambigu-
ously and that it would be possible to write a whole chapter, or
even more, on many of them. Additionally, as a result of this
ambiguity it would be possible to classify the terms within more
than one section of the following analysis, but for the sake of
clarity (even if not total accuracy) little of this is undertaken
below. The prefixes themselves constitute at least ten different
major facets of education, each having a number of individual,
or more complex, manifestations and these are: the content of

education; the learners; the life cycle of the learners; education
and its legal position; the level of education; the location of the
process; the methodology implied by the classification; the
explicit philosophy of the terminology; the providers of education; the apparent purpose of specific types of education. It
would also be possible to combine some of these types to refine
even more precisely the manifestations of the concept of education under discussion. Additionally, the term 'education' may
itself be used to refer to both the academic discipline or the
institution of education, but even in these instances it may be
more accurate to refer to the specific sub-discipline being
studied or the branch of the instituion being discussed.

The Content of Education

The content of education is the concern of curriculum studies
rather than to conceptual analysis of 'education' per se, so that
no attempt is made here to enter the realm of the curriculum.
Even so, the concept is frequently prefixed by terms that
specify areas of content but these rarely seem to relate to
specific academic disciplines, e.g. chemistry education, but
relate more specifically to whole areas of human life and, in most
instances, upon a number of disciplines, or sub-disciplines.
Examples from this category include: aesthetic education, affective
education, agricultural education, business education, citizen-
ship education, civic education, general education, health educa-
tion, international education, liberal education, moral education,
parenthood education, physical education, religious education,
sports education, technical education and trade union education.
In no instance do these prefixes specify the actual content of
the curriculum nor do they exclude the perspectives that a
variety of disciplines might have upon their area of concern,
rather they relate in a broad manner to specific areas/
institutions in society which may be the focus of an educational
process.

The Learners for Whom the Educational Process May be instituted

The definitions with which this chapter opened all contained
implicit references to the fact that education was for children.
While that proposition has been shown to be incorrect, it does
not preclude one branch of education being referred to as child
education, or as it is now frequently called 'initial education'.
By contrast to initial education, learners may be adults, so that
the term 'adult education' is also employed; although this is
often used with specific reference to local education authority
provision of liberal education for adults. Additionally, the term
may refer to the fact that the educational process should be
conducted in an adult manner within an environment suitable
for adults. Often 'adult education' is employed in contrast to
the term 'the education of adults' but further reference will be

made to this discussion in the next section of this chapter, so
that it will not be pursued here.

Within vocational education, the learners for whom the process
of education is provided are specified much more clearly. For
instance, an individual profession may be named in the form of
education, such as legal education, medical education, nurse
education or teacher education. By contrast, the position in the
occupational hierarchy may be employed as a point of reference:
labour education, management education, worker education.
Another form of education is often provided, by comparison, for
employees which also reflects the stage that they have reached
in their occupational career, e.g. pre-retirement education. (In
the United Kingdom the Pre-Retirement Association has been a
leading exponent of this form of education.) It is hardly surprising that, because of the increasing number of elderly in
the population, the concept of retirement education has also
appeared in more recent years.

Finally, the learners may be specified in another way, with
distinct groups being the focus of the education. Hence in
countries receiving immigrants, immigrant education has arisen.
Additionally, in America especially, alumni education has been
developed, being the education provided by colleges for their
former students.

The Learners' Life Cycle and Education

Reference to child and adult education in the previous section
indicates how difficult it is to separate the complex phenomenon
of education into discrete branches. Yet education is provided
for the whole of the life cycle, so that lifelong education is a
term used to cover this process. However, the term lifelong
education refers not only to the whole of the life cycle but it
is also used to embrace all forms of education, whether general
or vocational, provided throughout the whole of life. Since
education is a lifelong process, the term 'lifelong' might be seen
to be superfluous to the concept of 'education' but since so much
emphasis has been placed upon initial education for the young,
thereby distorting the total analysis, lifelong has become a
necessary prefix. But the actual stages of the life cycle are
actually specified: pre-school (or nursery) education is followed
by: primary education, junior education, secondary education,
adolescent education, education of young adults, vocational
education, adult education, retirement education and, even,
death education.

Education and its Legal Position

In many societies of the world, attendance at school for initial
education is required by law for children. Hence the terms
compulsory and post-compulsory education have gained currency
in usage. Additionally, the term further education also has the

connotation of post-school and post-compulsory education.

The Level of the Educational Provision

Primary and secondary education almost imply the level of education rather than the phase in the life cycle of the education. Yet there are a number of terms that relate education directly to the assumed level of its content: basic education, elementary education, remedial education, intermediate education, further education, advanced education and higher education may all be included in this list. Another way by which the level of education is often implied is by prefixing the term with either academic or non-academic. The former is often regarded as having either a vocational purpose or being validated in some way so that upon successful completion the learner receives some form of certification, whereas the latter sometimes carries connotation of liberal education or leisure time education for purposes of enjoyment.

In the professions, the level of education might be specified in terms of basic and post-basic, or initial and post-initial (or continuing) education. Post-basic education is usually a form of in-service education, for which secondment is often granted to the person, in order to pursue further education within the individual's own branch of a profession or to prepare for transfer to another branch of the profession upon successful completion of the process.

Location of Education

Education usually occurs in schools, colleges, polytechnics and universities, so that each of these locations has been used as a prefix to describe types of education.

It is hardly surprising, therefore, that post-school education, etc. has been employed to describe a form that relates to continuation education or alumni education and/or other forms of education implicit in the sequence from school to university noted above. By contrast, out-of-school and home education have been employed to relate to forms of education that occur outside of educational institutions. Similarly, extramural and extension education refer to types of education in which the educational institution, or organisation seeks to extend its educational provision by offering education in the wider community.

Community education, itself, has sometimes been employed as a synonymous term to extra-mural, or out-of-school, education. However, it has also assumed at least two other major connotations: using school or university premises for the education of anybody in the community, irrespective of age or ability, who wishes to pursue a course of education. Additionally, the term has assumed a more radical meaning in which it refers to the process whereby people may be educated to be aware of themselves and their social and legal rights and, thereafter, acting upon the knowledge in order to produce social change in the community.

The Methodology Implied by the Process

It was suggested earlier that adult education, as a term, might refer to an adult form of method underlying the educational process, so that there are prefixes to the process that relate to types of education. For instance, in a similar manner the terms formal, informal and non-formal may be employed as prefixes to education to classify types of education.

Another prefix to the term that has become more widely used in recent years is 'distance education'. (This term refers, of course, to the fact that the teacher and the learner are separated by distance, an obstacle which might be overcome by correspondence or by other technical media.) Correspondence courses have been a well tried educational method for many years but distance education has really been popularised in the United Kingdom since the founding of the Open University. More recently this method of education has been introduced by a number of educational institutions and a growing number of professions are also considering introducing distance education into some of their post-basic courses. It is interesting to note how correspondence courses were often used as a low-status method of entry into the professions, but one which had been successively reduced. However, with the growing interest in distance education it is being reintroduced, but now at a post-basic level.

Explicit Philosophy in the Terminology

Obviously many philosophical ideas have been implicated in a number of the terms commented upon in this section, although little attempt has been made to draw out these implications here. Yet there are some terms that do make explicit reference to philosophical arguments. Remedial education, noted earlier, implicitly has reference to the idea of compensatory education and second-chance education. Perhaps the adult basic education scheme is the most explicit compensatory form of education that has occurred in the United Kingdom. Yet similar philosophical perspectives are contained in terms like comprehensive education and integrated education, in which people of all races, religions, abilities and of both sexes may participate in the same educational process. Similarly, the term universal education implies equal rights in education for everybody. Mass education also refers to the fact that most people may be participants in, or recipients of, the educational process although it does not necessarily contain the same explicit philosophical position. By contrast, open education does contain implicit ideas of education being accessible to all people irrespective of personal, social or, even, educational prerequisites.

Lifelong education may also be regarded as containing a specifically philosophical perspective, but not all would agree with this. Yet terms frequently used in a similar manner to this, i.e. community education, continuing education, recurrent education, may reflect philosophical ideals. The latter two terms will be referred to in the third section of this chapter, so that no further reference will be made to them now.

The Providers of the Educational Process

This is rather similar in type to some of the previous sub-sections so that it is unnecessary to give it a great deal of space. Among the providers are the state, professions and trade unions, so that each may prefix the term 'education'. However, the terms 'independent' and 'private' contain both reference to the provision of the process and to the fact that specific ideological perspectives may also be adduced from the terms.

Apparent Purpose of the Type of Education

This sub-section in no way impinges upon the discussion of the aims of education in the third chapter of this book, it merely reflects the fact that some of the prefixes to the terms indicate the purpose of the branch of education to which reference is being made. Hence the terms, careers education, general education, industrial education, social education and vocational education all contain within their title specific reference to purpose.

This classification of branches of education is by no means complete, neither is it intended to be. It intentionally omits all reference to 'good' or 'bad' education, although later there is discussion about the relationship between education and values. The only intention underlying this present discussion has been to illustrate the complexity of education per se and to suggest that the process underlying all of these types has a similarity which may be viewed as a common stem. If this is accepted, then it is claimed that the definition of the stem formulated in the first section of this chapter is applicable to each of the branches, bearing in mind the modification that would have to be made in order to account for the meaning explicit in the prefix.

Not all of these branches of education are relevant to a discussion of professional education and the final section of this chapter concentrates upon those branches of education that specifically relate to the education of professionals.

PROFESSIONAL EDUCATION AND DIFFERING BRANCHES OF EDUCATION

In the previous section of this chapter it was demonstrated that education is a diverse phenomenon and it is now necessary to relate some of the branches of education discussed to professional education. Initially, the concept of lifelong education will be examined since, in many ways, it is the most meaningful of all within the philosophical framework, and it will be followed by a discussion on the education of adults/adult education debate. Thereafter, it is necessary to examine briefly the idea of professional basic or initial education, continuing education and recurrent education and the way in which they relate to in-service and post-basic education.

Lifelong Education

Dave (1976: 34) defines this as 'the process of accomplishing personal, social and professional development throughout the life-span of individuals in order to enhance the quality of both individuals and their collectivities'. This definition is rather unwieldy, probably because it includes specific aims but, nevertheless, it serves to illustrate how some scholars have viewed the idea. Nevertheless, the definition of education formulated earlier in this chapter can be slightly modified in order to relate it specifically to this aspect of education: lifelong education is the provision of any planned series of incidents throughout the lifespan of individuals which have a humanistic basis, and are directed towards learning and understanding.

Viewed from this perspective it is clear that the original concept of education has merely been adapted to make it meaningful within the context of lifelong education. Hence lifelong education is merely one manifestation of the original concept and, in this sense, it is possible to agree with Lawson (1982) that there is nothing new in the concept. However, the fact that lifelong education has obtained so much credibility at the present time is hardly surprising since social change and the explosion of knowledge have been so rapid. Not all scholars, however, view this change in the understanding of education as necessarily desirable. Illich and Verne (1976: 14) see some potential problems:

> Just as suffering has been medicalized, existence has been scholarized, and even become the subject for an apprenticeship. The medical profession in forcing people to be born and die in hospital, succeeded in inculcating the idea that life is a disease. Now professional educators, through the institution of permanent education, succeed in convincing men of their permanent incompetence. The ultimate success of the schooling instrument is the extension of its monopoly, first of all to youth, then to every age and, finally, to all areas.

Clearly the fears of Illich and Verne are real, and the bureau-cratisation and institutionalisation of education may result in the type of 'global classroom' that they fear. Nevertheless, there is considerable evidence (see Tough 1971, Hiemstra 1975, Gross 1977, among others) to suggest that lifelong learning is a process that many embark upon because of their humanity rather than because of the demands made upon them from the wider society. Yet Illich and Verne serve to remind all educators that only the learner is intrinsic to the process of lifelong education.

Recently, Finniston (1980: 206ff) has argued that lifelong learning is important for professionals, and among the recommen-dations of the Committee of Inquiry into the Engineering Pro-fession was one that indicated that the professional engineer should be a lifelong learner. Dennis (1980: 187ff) also sees the significance of lifelong education for the professions and he traces the influence of school education, as well as successive education, on the practice of employers.

Nevertheless, in this discussion, lifelong learning is as important as lifelong education. The latter is about the provision of educational opportunity while the former relates both to the humanity of the learner and to his motivation to learn. It will be argued later in this book that the desire to learn throughout the whole of the period of professional practice is intrinsic to professionalism: a point with which Houle (1980: 84) agrees:

> it is probable that the way in which a basic professional programme might enhance later competence would be by ensur-ing the fact that, during the years spent in the (professional) school's sub-culture, the students' personal commitment to lifelong learning is firmly established . . .

It is, therefore, suggested that lifelong learning is fundamental to professionalism and that therefore lifelong education provides a conceptual framework within which professional education may be located. Since the learners in this area of education are also adults, it is now necessary to explore the relationship between the term adult education and professional education.

Adult Education

It was suggested in the previous section that the term adult education has many varying meanings and it is really beyond the scope of this study to embark upon a discussion of these; nevertheless, these will be referred to here briefly. The term 'adult education' is frequently used to indicate the liberal education provided by local education authorities for adults. However, it may also relate to an educational process undertaken, or conducted, in an adult manner: this has been discussed more fully by Wiltshire (1976). But these two approaches both call into question the word 'adult': in the former, it refers to those who have left initial education and are regarded as adults on account of their chronological age but, in the second, adult refers to a form of maturity. Patterson (1979) also concludes that 'adult' should really relate only to age, whereas Knowles (1980) emphasises the element of maturity a little more. Since it is difficult to assess maturity it has not necessarily been stipulated as an essential quality for a candidate to have when embarking upon training but by contrast a specific minimum age of entry is usually required. The concept of adult education in this context may be understood in terms of the education of those who have attained at least a specific chronological age. Hence, professional education may be understood as fitting within the framework of the education of adults and, perhaps, it would be less confusing conceptually to locate it here than within other explanations of adult education. Even so, in the chapter concerned with educational processes, further reference will be made to the idea that professional education should be undertaken, or conducted, in an adult manner.

Professional Basic Education

This form of education reflects the intra-generational definitions of education that a new recruit to the profession receives prior to commencing practice. In some professions it has now become a long period spent studying in higher education – as long as six or seven years in some instances. This progressive lengthening of professional education and training has led Houle (1980: 84) to state that the 'professional school must separate essential from non-essential knowledge' and the authors of the Faure Report (1972: 230) too argue that:

> we should endeavour to reduce the length of studies to acquire a given qualification (without reducing standards) by perfecting teaching methods, speeding the learning process, carefully selecting the knowledge to be acquired, and combining study with work, either directly or in successive phases.

While it is not the intention here to discuss criteria for the selection of curriculum content it is important to point out that the actual length of initial education need have no relationship to the level of professionalism of the practitioners. However, as Houle (1980: 84) points out, there is a trend to concentrate on the theoretical perspectives of the profession during initial education since 'on the job training' and 'tutelage' are given during practice especially in the legal and engineering professions in America. This is a point to which future reference will be made since not all professions divide their initial education and training in quite this manner, nor do they all regard it as desirable.

Continuing and Recurrent Education

These two terms relate in specific ways to both in-service and post-basic education in the context of professional education and yet there is confusion about the meaning of both. It is, therefore, important to recognise this fact and to attempt to clarify it. This is a difficult task since writers on these two concepts tend to disagree about their definitions.

Apps (1979: 67) cites an article, written in 'Adult Leadership' (1955), which offered nine different definitions of continuing education, many of which relate it to education continuing into adult life. From the Open University 'Report on Continuing Education' (1976: 19) the following definition emerges:

> Continuing education is thus understood . . . to include all
> learning opportunities which are taken up after full-time com-
> pulsory schooling has ceased . . .

Unfortunately, the Advisory Council for Adult and Continuing Education offered no definition in its paper 'Towards Continuing Education' (1979: 7) but rather equated it with lifelong learning and recurrent education. Nevertheless, in the field of professional education, the term continuing education has assumed significance in as much as it is recognised that continuing learning or education is essential to good practice and that the basic professional education is no longer sufficient for a lifetime of practice.

Recurrent education is claimed by one of its exponents (Houghton 1974: 6) to be 'the first new idea in education this century' which is rather an exaggerated claim for the idea. It has been defined as 'a comprehensive' educational strategy for all post-compulsory or post-basic education, the essential characteristic of which is the distribution of education over the total life span of the individual in a recurring way, i.e. in alternation with other activities, principally with work, but also with leisure and retirement (OECD, 1973: 24). Griffin (1978: 3) clearly summarises the differences between the two concepts of continuing and recurrent education.

> The social policy of continuing education has evolved from
> the liberal-democratic tradition of adult education itself, and
> it is concerned that the education system should serve the
> lifelong needs of people in all sectors of society, particularly
> those in relatively disadvantaged groups . . . The social
> policy of recurrent education is much more of an alternative
> to the existing education system than a response to its inad-
> equacies and failings: it is inclined to a political view of
> educational institutions, stressing the way in which they
> create and re-inforce inequality . . .

Less radical writers on recurrent education than Houghton tend to view it as a strategy for lifelong education (OECD 1973)

so that confusion does reign between these concepts. Since the
two concepts partially overlap it is considered preferable in this
context to treat continuing education as the term more applicable
to the education of professionals. Indeed, this term is more
frequently employed in this way and it may be defined within the
framework of the definition of education adopted in this chapter
as any planned series of incidents, beyond initial education,
having a humanistic basis, directed towards the participant(s)'
learning and understanding.

Continuing education in the professions may have a number of
purposes including giving practitioners the opportunity to
update their knowledge of new developments in their profession,
or to undertake an additional course so that the participants may
move from one branch of the occupation to another, or to acquire
additional specialist knowledge. It may be taken full-time, part-
time or even through a combination of these, with, in some
instances, a distance education element added. Clearly the professions have recognised the need for continuing education,
with for example, the James Report recommending school teachers
should have the opportunity of continuing education and the
Finniston Report making the same suggestion for engineers.

This section has discussed some of the central terms in professional education and it has sought to locate them within the
wider framework of education. It has not sought to define
concepts in a categorical fashion since it is recognised that a
wide diversity of opinion exists about many of these. At the
same time, it has related elements of professional education to
those broader educational concepts, which reflects a tendency
in professional education to see itself within the wider educational
milieu.

CONCLUSION

This chapter began by seeking to discover a definition of education that would be applicable to all the different branches
and manifestations of the concept. It concluded that education
is any planned series of incidents, having a humanistic basis,
directed towards the participant(s)' learning and understanding.
This was shown to be applicable to the many branches and manifestations of education. Some of these were discussed in order
to clarify the complexity of the phenomenon and, finally, some
of these more specific types of education were related to elements
of professional education. The manner in which the concept of
education has changed has been apparent throughout the discussion, with many of the earlier concepts of education being
shown to refer to one facet of education only. It is now important
that the concepts surrounding the word 'profession' and already
used in this opening chapter should be explored in greater depth.

Professionals *profess*. They profess to know better than others
the nature of certain matters, and to know better than their
clients what ails them or their affairs. This is the essence of
the professional idea and the professional claim. From it flow
many consequences . . .

(Hughes 1963: 656)

The mere fact that the practitioners of any occupation or craft
profess anything, indicates the origins of the word within a
religious context. Nowadays the word, like the society in which
it is employed, has been secularised. Yet beneath the kudos
implicit within the word, there still lies the idea that this status
is founded upon a greater degree of knowledge, skill or something that ordinary occupations do not have. Hence it is hardly
surprising, in an achievement-orientated society, that the status
of profession is both esteemed and aspired after by many other
occupations. Herein lies one of the major difficulties in seeking
to discuss the education of professionals - precisely what
occupations come within the ambit of this term? Many publications
have appeared in which this problem is discussed but it is hardly
the purpose of this chapter to review all the literature. It is,
however, intended to present a conceptual framework within
which the terms may be placed in the remainder of this book and,
in order to do this, it is necessary to refer to some of this
literature - most of which stems from sociologists who have
investigated the phenomenon of high-status occupations.

A cursory examination of this literature reveals four core
words used with varying meanings, by different writers:
profession, professionalisation, professional and professionalism.
At the outset, therefore, it is necessary to clarify the way in
which these terms are employed and, before even this is undertaken, the terms are subdivided: the former two are used in
relation to the occupation and the others to the practitioner.
Even this broad classification does not find universal agreement
among the writers on the subject, for Houle (1980: 10, 34)
employs the term 'professionalization' with implications of corporate improvement within the occupation, whereas Elliott (1972:
10) relates 'professionalism' to the social structure. Many other
similar examples could be cited of scholars who employ these
concepts in a slightly different manner.

It might be queried at this juncture why the emphasis on
definition is so important since once again there appears to be a

family of words which is almost indefinable. While such a position might be tenable, it is necessary to note that since there are no agreed usages of the terms it is important to specify how they will be employed in this study. This is not to claim that such definitions are, therefore, any more applicable than any others. The four words will now be discussed in turn.

PROFESSION

Among the numerous attempts to define this concept three of the most well known are noted here. Carr-Saunders (1928 cited in Vollmer and Mills 1966: 4) claimed that a profession 'may perhaps be defined as an occupation based upon specialized intellectual study and training, the purpose of which is to supply skilled service or advice to others for a definite fee or salary'. More recently, Cogan (1953: 49) sought to reduce the number of characteristics of the occupation incorporated in the definition when he suggested initially that a profession is 'a vocation whose practice is founded upon an understanding of a theoretical structure of some department of learning or science'. Both of these definitions merely imply that professions are, in some manner, service occupations and, therefore, valuable to society. By contrast, Elliott (1972: 11) presented another perspective when he stated that 'a professional group controls a body of expert knowledge which is applied to specialist tasks'. Elliott does not signify that professions are not valuable to society but he does claim that professions control a valuable resource, such as knowledge. This might lead to corruption, dominance or self-seeking rather than to altruism and, hence, some analysts and social commentators have suggested that professions have selfishly sought to control valuable services in society. It may, therefore, be seen that no simple or agreed definition exists that might describe the characteristics of this occupational type, nor is there agreement about how these occupations may serve society.

Many attempts have been made to describe, rather than to define, the professions by their characteristics. Millerson (1964: 5) highlighted this when, reviewing the work of twenty-five writers on the professions, he listed twenty-three different occupational traits that they attributed to them. Since the publication of his work, other authors have also endeavoured to employ this perspective (e.g. Hickson and Thomas 1969; Leggatt 1970). Indeed, more recently, the prominent American educationalist, Houle (1980: 34ff) has suggested a slightly different variation on this theme. He has maintained that there are at least fourteen characteristics that can be associated with the dynamic process of corporate improvement within the occupation (professionalisation). These characteristics are: definition of the occupation's functions; mastery of theoretical knowledge; capacity to solve problems; use of practical know-

ledge; self-enhancement; formal training; credentialing; creation
of a sub-culture; legal reinforcement, public acceptance; ethical
practice; penalties, relations to other vocations; relations to the
users of the service. While Houle places these characteristics
along a number of different axes - conceptual, performance and
collective identity characteristics - he does not really define the
concept of profession itself. Yet no approach that seeks to describe a phenomenon may ever succeed in defining it and Johnson
(1972) has rightly pointed out that the procedure of listing
traits without a theoretical framework is dangerous because
characteristics may be added to or subtracted from any existing
list by any author without any theoretical rationale. Such is the
confusion in and profusion of definition that Vollmer and Mills
(1966: vii) use the term 'profession' as an 'ideal type' rather
than to arbitrate as to whether an occupation is a profession,
or not. Even so, it might be claimed, it is necessary to be able
to define the ideal type, so that some meaning is given to the
word. Perhaps it would be true to suggest that few commentators
on those occupations to which the status of 'profession' is usually
attributed would disagree that they are occupations which seek
in some ways both the mastery of an identifiable body of knowledge and the control of its application in practice. This
definition should be regarded as a working definition providing
a theoretical basis for the ensuing discussion. Nevertheless,
numerous implications and connotations are apparent, many of
which will be explored in later chapters of this book, but two
must be recognised at the outset and these are discussed briefly:
the concept implies that some occupations have power and that
the term itself covers a number of different occupations in various
stages of their development.

Power and the Professions

Occupations whose practitioners have mastery over an area of
knowledge have a degree of power by virtue of their expertise,
but many professions have sought and obtained legislation that
disqualifies untrained or unregistered personnel from practising.
This has resulted in many occupations issuing a code of ethics
of professional practice so that clients may know the standard
and commitment that they should receive from a registered practitioner. By contrast, the mastery of knowledge and the control
of its practice has resulted in certain occupations and practitioners exercising a degree of power in society that has led to
certain social analysts questioning the idealism of the service
ethic. Illich et al. (1977: 22), among others, have suggested
that this control over knowledge has resulted in the dominance
of the servant:

> The dominant professional provides jury or legislature with
> his own and fellow-initiates' global opinion, rather than with
> factual self-limiting evidence and specific skill. Armed with

an aura of divine authority, he calls for the suspension of
the hearsay rule and inevitably undermines the rule of law.
Thus, one sees how democratic power is subverted by an un-
questioned assumption of an all-embracing professionalism.

In a less sweeping manner, Eliot Freidson (1970) could analyse
the American medical profession in terms of 'professional dominance' and claim that such dominance is an analytical key to the
present inadequacy of the health services.

It must be recognised that professional occupations have frequently aspired to this powerful position while constantly claiming that they are offering a service, one which they have, in
fact, frequently given. Nevertheless, the significance of this
discussion is merely to demonstrate that professions are not
necessarily 'good' in themselves and that the power that results
from control of the application of knowledge has not always been
as altruistic as certain professional associations might claim.

A Composite Concept

Professions, according to Elliott (1972: 14), are of two historical
types: status profession and occupational profession. The former
he defines as ones which 'were relatively unimportant in the
organization of work and community services but occupied a niche
high in systems of social stratification' while the latter are 'based
on the specialisation of knowledge and tasks'. While he regards
these as being within an historical dimension, it is possible to
view them within a contemporary framework since medicine,
ministry and nursing may be viewed as a status while the actual
type of work undertaken, surgeon, parish priest and district
nurse, may be regarded as the occupation (Jarvis 1975). These
terms will be thus employed in this book.

Elliott's recognition that professions change in relation to
specific social situations has been reflected in a number of
studies. Reiss (1955) for instance, proposed five different types
of profession in contemporary, industrial society.

(i)   Old established professions - founded upon the study of
       a branch of learning, e.g. medicine.
(ii) New professions - founded upon new disciplines, e.g.
       chemists, social scientists.
(iii) Semi-professions - based upon technical practice and
       knowledge, e.g. nurses, teachers, social workers.
(iv) Would-be professions - familiarity with modern practices
       in business, etc. distinguish this group who aspire to
       professional status, e.g. personnel directors, sales
       directors, engineers, etc.
(v)   Marginal professions - based upon technical skill, e.g.
       technicians, draughtsmen.

It will be noticed in the above typology that each of these

types is classified in relation to a body of knowledge and its
application and, while the location of different occupations within
this typology might be disputable, the composite nature of the
occupations which might claim professional status is less so!
Reiss studied the occupational mobility of individuals through
this hierarchy of occupational types, but it is just as easy to
recognise the process whereby an occupation itself moves through
this progression. It was this process that led Hughes (1958:
45) to state:

> in my studies I passed from the false question, 'Is this
> occupation a profession?' to a more fundamental one, 'What
> are the circumstances in which the people in an occupation
> attempt to turn it into a profession, and themselves into pro-
> fessional people?' and 'What are the steps by which they
> attempt to bring about identification with their valued model?'

Therefore, the process of change, professionalisation (and even
deprofessionalisation) has evoked considerable enquiry and it is
now necessary to examine this second, more dynamic concept.

PROFESSIONALISATION

> the concept of 'professionalization' may be used to refer
> to the dynamic process whereby many occupations can be
> observed to change crucial characteristics in the direction of
> a 'profession' even though some of these may not move very
> far in this direction. (Vollmer and Mills 1966: vii-viii)

A number of commentators have sought to isolate and describe
this pilgrimage towards professional status; the ideas of three
of them will be briefly discussed in this section - Caplow (1954),
Greenwood (1957), Wilensky (1964).
Caplow suggested that the first stage in this transition is the
establishment of a professional association, followed by a change
in occupational title, for example undertaker to funeral director.
Thirdly, a code of ethics is published which portrays the 'social
utility' of the occupation, which is followed by legislation
restricting specific practices to the occupation. He points out
that concurrently with this go the development of training
facilities and the control of admission to training, qualification
and entry into the profession. Thus the occupation controls
every aspect of training and practice through various sub-
committees of its professional association.
A few years later, Greenwood sought to make even more
explicit this formulation of Caplow's. He claimed that there are
five attributes of a profession (note the criticisms of the trait
approach discussed earlier): Greenwood recognised that non-
professional occupations possess some of these attributes, but
to a lesser degree than the **professions**. However, he argued

that occupations may be located along a continuum with the professions possessing these attributes to a greater degree and the non-professions to a lesser one. Greenwood, writing about social workers, suggests that social work will move along this continuum of professionalisation and in the process this will incur 'novel relationships with clients, colleagues, agency, community and other professions' (cited in Vollmer and Mills 1966: 19).

Caplow suggested that the process was apparent and Greenwood highlighted it for social work, but Wilensky claimed that the process of professionalisation was one upon which everyone could embark. He suggests that, while the sequence is not invariant, there is some form of progression and it is necessary for the occupations to:

(i) start doing full-time that which needs doing;
(ii) establish a training school which, if not at the outset, later seeks to integrate with universities;
(iii) form a professional association which seeks:
    (a) self-conscious definition of the core tasks of the occupation;
    (b) a cosmopolitan perspective to the practice of the occupation; and
    (c) to compete with neighbouring occupations in order to establish the area of exclusive competence.
(iv) seek legal support for the protection of the job territory and to publish a code of ethics to indicate the commitment of the practitioner. This results in control of licensing and certification;
(v) publish a formal code of ethics, eliminating the unqualified and reducing internal competition whilst assuring the public that the profession will serve its needs.

From this summary of Wilensky's position it may be seen that the process of professionalisation involves changes in the occupational structure, so that it reflects whatever professional model the elite of the occupation espouse. This process, whatever model of change is adopted, certainly reflects the social reality of occupations seeking to have the title 'profession' attributed to them as well as ascribing it to themselves, yet the sequence of the progression is not so well defined in practice.

Despite this criticism, a number of important points occur in this analysis for the educationalist. Once an occupation is full-time then it may seek to establish a training school which, if not already linked, may later seek to establish relationships with universities. While Wilensky's discussion is relevant to America, it would certainly reflect the reality of the present situation in Britain where many different occupations are establishing links with universities, polytechnics and other educational institutions. The majority of Reiss' old established and new professions have faculties, schools or departments in universities and polytechnics. Some of the semi-professions, like teaching, which have had relations with universities, have more recently established links with other institutions of higher education and no longer train their recruits in monotechnic training colleges. Branches of nursing, e.g. district nursing, have also sought to move from schools of nursing to educational institutions. Indeed, the 'would be' and marginal professions are also establishing much of their training within the wider educational institutions.

Another factor concerning the process of professionalisation that requires consideration here is the extent to which occupations actually achieve the end-product of the movement along the continuum of professionalisation. It is doubtful whether, with the increase in research and the knowledge explosion, this will occur since before it does, further specialisation tends to happen which will result in segmentation within the profession. Bucher and Strauss (1961) developed the idea of 'professions as loose amalgamations of segments pursuing different objectives in different manners and more or less delicately held together under a common name at a particular period in history' (cited in Vollmer and Mills 1966: 186). Their analysis is similar to that discussed earlier in which the amalgamation of segments may be regarded as the status profession, i.e. medicine, ministry, nursing, whereas the individual segments, general practice, chaplaincy, district nursing, may be seen as the occupation which is endeavouring to professionalise. This process of segmentation has been inhibited in some areas and in social work, for instance, the Seebohm Report (1968) recommended that 'each local authority in England and Wales should establish a single social work agency to provide virtually all the authority's social work services' (Smith 1978: 14) and, as a result, 'most social services departments assigned to their social workers a generic role, which included a full share of routine and practical tasks (Irvine 1978: 104).

If training for any occupations were to change and become more practically orientated and less knowledge-based (values that will be discussed later) it might be argued that in occupational terms the process of professionalisation had been reversed and occupational deprofessionalisation had occurred. Such deprofessionalisation might have occurred within branches of other status professions, such as general practice in medicine and the parish ministry. Nevertheless, it may be recognised from this discussion that whether segmentation and professionalisation or deprofessionalisation occurs, the process itself has a direct relationship to the curriculum of training. Indeed, the philosophical issues underlying this are even greater since among the aims of training will almost certainly occur recognition of the state of change within the occupational profession itself and what the elite within the profession, or those outside of it who control it, seek to achieve for it in the future. Thus Hughes could ask his searching questions about why 'people in an occupation attempt to turn it into a profession and themselves into professional people' (see above).

PROFESSIONAL

'Professional' as a noun, in opposition to the term 'amateur', applies to one who receives emoluments for the performance of his occupational tasks. He is also one who practises a profession and one who is regarded as an 'expert' since he has mastery of a specific branch of learning. These latter two meanings constitute the present concern since the first one is merely a figment of common speech and a truism. The second, however, makes the assumption that one who practises an occupation which has achieved professional status is automatically the master of whatever branch of learning the professional occupation claims to control. However, the research by Rogers (1962) on innovation within medicine suggests that this is a false equation. Not all practitioners actually master new developments in the area of learning upon which their professional occupation is founded and, therefore, they expose themselves to the critical judgement of their fellow-practitioners.

It is suggested here, therefore, that the professional is one who continually seeks the mastery of the branch of learning upon which his occupation is based, so that he may offer a service to his client. This definition clearly implies a positive evaluation of a professional. But it is recognised that the conflict caused by seeking to be the master of an academic branch of learning and endeavouring to serve clients may result in one or other of these aspects suffering. Hence the concept remains an 'ideal type' to which some practitioners approximate.

In order to be the master of a branch of learning it is essential for a practitioner to continue his learning after initial education and some professions have institutionalised continuing education. Thus Williams and Huntley (1979: 44) claim that:

> Continuing education, voluntary or mandatory, is a requirement likely to become universal for professionals within the next decade.

Already some professions, such as midwifery, insist that practitioners can only remain members of the profession provided that they undertake a refresher course at specified intervals. Yet even refresher courses do not guarantee that practitioners remain masters of the branch of learning upon which their occupation is based, so that the concept of professional is used to refer to the practitioner who seeks to be the master of the knowledge upon which his occupation is founded. But this may be regarded as too narrow a conception since the practitioner has to use the knowledge within the performance of his duties, so that the concept is expanded a little to embrace both the mastery and application of that knowledge and is defined as: one who endeavours to have mastery of and to apply effectively that knowledge upon which his occupation is based. Not all who practise the professional occupations may be regarded as professionals but it is possible to discover professionals in occupations which do not have professional status. Nevertheless, this analysis must necessarily restrict itself to philosophical issues surrounding the education and training of recruits and members of occupations that have the social esteem and recognition as professions.

PROFESSIONALISM

Once again this term has two meanings, relating to two of the interpretations of professional discussed above: commitment to the occupational organisation, and dedication to being a master of the knowledge and a skilful provider of service stemming from the knowledge upon which the occupation is based. From an ideological perspective Freidson (1970: 151) defines professionalism as 'commitment to professional ideals and career . . . expressed in attitudes, ideas and beliefs'. He goes on to claim that:

> Operative professionalism is thus constituted by commitment to occupationally defined knowledge and technique and occupationally defined public service, to a particular occupation's view of correct knowledge and ethicality. (1970: 153)

Since many occupational professions are research orientated the knowledge upon which the occupation is based expands and this introduces a dynamic into the situation which is lacking in the above quotation. Nevertheless, the closed perspective apparent in this quotation is perhaps the logical outcome of an occupation seeking to demarcate for the sake of control. From such a limited perspective, it is hardly surprising that there often occurs an overemphasis on peer-reference, to the exclusion of client reference, which may result in the professional failing to serve the client adequately and, consequently, being exposed to the criticisms of imperiousness, etc. which Illich and others level at the professionals.

Additionally, it must be recognised here that the term 'professionalism' may be used to relate to the level of proficiency of the practitioner rather than to his ideology. Indeed, this latter usage of the word is much more in accord with the definition of professional suggested in the previous section. The level of proficiency may result from the individual practitioner's commitment to being the master of the knowledge upon which his occupation is founded and to providing an effective service to his client. Nevertheless, this proficiency reflects an attitude towards his occupation which demands that the practitioner con-

tinue to learn about recent developments in both the knowledge
and application of that knowledge to the occupational setting.
It is an attitude that enjoins the practitioner to be a lifelong
learner rather than a reluctant recruit to continuing education
provided by either the occupational profession or by a local
institution of further or higher education. This attitude towards
knowledge and service is directly contrary to that of institutionalised continuing education which Illich and Verne (1976: 20)
claim 'will transform society into an enormous plant-sized classroom' in which everyone is imprisoned.

CONCLUDING DISCUSSION

Thus far, it has been argued that the term 'profession' is an
ideal type so that there is no agreed conceptual basis by which
it is possible to determine whether, or not, an occupation is a
profession. Rather the term 'status profession' is suggested to
refer to those families of occupations generally ascribed as having
the status of profession while 'occupational profession' relates
to those occupations engaged in the process of professionalisation.
Clearly, the high-status professions are difficult to enter whereas
the lower-status ones are more readily accessible. Hence Goode
(1957) likened the professions to communities into which entry
was difficult. Etzioni (1967) actually differentiated the training
period for recruits into the professions and those into the semi-
professions, claiming that in America entry into the 'fully fledged'
professions demanded a period of at least five years training
whereas entry into the semi-profession required only three years
training. However long the period, it is clear that the status of
the occupation will be reflected in both the length and location of
its training, the awards given on completion of training and the
difficulty of access to the training. All of these are issues that
demand consideration later in this study.
  Throughout this chapter it has been apparent that at the
foundation of every occupation claiming professional status is
knowledge and its application. Therefore the relationships
between mastering and applying knowledge, education and
training, theory and practice all need exploration in the following chapters. However, the concept of knowledge itself and its
relation to the segmentation of different occupational professions
requires exploration, since there may be attempts to hold segments together (with a core curriculum) in training, interdisciplinary study days, etc. By contrast, other pressures may
be put upon curriculum planners to ensure that the precise
knowledge base of the occupational profession is taught, for
example health visiting knowledge rather than nursing knowledge
or nursing knowledge rather than medical knowledge. Thus the
relationship between the aims of professional training, the concept of knowledge and the curriculum for the education and
training of recruits needs exploration.

During the discussion on professionalism, it was clear that the ideological interpretation of the concept implies degrees of commitment to the occupation. Such commitment may be the result of the hidden curriculum in training; professional socialisation is clearly an important factor, especially where the recruits are trained in residential institutions and in relative isolation from the wider academic community. Hence the relationship between indoctrination, socialisation and training requires consideration. Indeed the relationship between the latter two concepts requires exploration in relation to the concepts of 'knowing that', and 'knowing how', and in relation to the knowledge and application of that knowledge in the occupational setting.

These opening two chapters have attempted to set the framework within which the remainder of this book will be placed. The next chapter examines the aims of professional education.

British educators, claims Davies (1976: 11), 'have been more interested in defining aims than in studying objectives, while American teachers have been willing to think in terms of concrete objectives'. While this assertion might be valid, it certainly reflects the tenor of this chapter which is concerned with the philosophical basis of the education of professionals and as Davies (1976: 13) goes on to state, aims tend 'to be broadly philosophical, if not timeless in . . . general applicability'. While no eternal verity will necessarily result from this chapter, its underlying rationale is to investigate the general shape and direction of the education of professionals.

Yet it might be claimed that the aims of professional education are self-evident, since it is clear that by the end of their period of training new recruits to a profession should be competent practitioners in their chosen occupation. However, it will be argued that this assertion of self-evidence, while not necessarily incorrect in itself, is neither complete nor very meaningful. Other factors, for instance, should be taken into consideration including: the nature of the process of education itself; the requirements of the wider society; the needs of the profession and the demands of practice; the learners themselves. Consideration of these factors gives rise to a discussion of the relationship between needs, wants and demands in the education and training of professionals. It is important, therefore, that all of these ideas are explored in more detail, so that each is now considered in turn and, thereafter, a concluding discussion draws together the points raised.

TO PRODUCE A COMPETENT PRACTITIONER

The aim of professional education is to produce competent practitioners, so claims the self-evident assertion. Yet this assertion is over-simplistic since, initially, two queries arise that lead to further questions: why should the practitioner be competent?; what is competency?

Why Should the Practitioner be Competent?

In the first instance this question might appear senseless - but not so! Indeed, it might have less relevance if all practitioners in occupations that claim professional status were actually competent, but the existence of professional disciplinary bodies and the occasional report in the media indicate that even practitioners in occupations having the highest social status at least occasionally fall short of competence. Some might consider that this is only to be expected since everyone is human, yet the degree of competency/incompetency in a profession is unknown, since once a practitioner has passed the qualifying examinations and is safely installed within his occupational niche, he has considerable freedom unless he makes catastrophic mistakes. If a practitioner is relatively incompetent, his professional colleagues may be aware of it and criticise him among themselves but their code of professional ethics would hinder them from doing this before his clients. Hence, an incompetent practitioner may be left to practise his 'quackery' (Hughes 1958) and this may satisfy his clients. If incompetence occurs in practice and the practitioner makes a living and satisfies his clients, why should he seek to be competent and why should competency be claimed as the end-product of the process of education and training?

Perhaps the beginnings of an answer to these questions lies in the point made earlier about everyone being human, since Schumacher (1977: 58) had claimed that:

> Education for good work is quite impossible. For how can we distinguish good work from bad work if human life on Earth has no meaning, no purpose? The word 'good' presupposes an aim . . .

While Schumacher's metaphysical response to these questions may not appeal to everyone, it is important that this discussion should not be avoided by superficial comments about the aims of professional education. Either the question is answered by reference to the nature of a profession and professionalism or else it gains credibility from the nature of humanity itself. Yet these possibilities are not entirely distinct since the word 'profess' originally had a religious meaning that has since been lost as the word, in common with many others, has become secularised. Nevertheless, many writers, such as Goode (1973) have claimed that service is one of the foundation stones of a profession and, therefore, a service ethic (altruism) is inherent in professionalism. But a practitioner in a professional occupation may not be committed to this ethic, yet still seek to serve his clients competently because he fears the disciplinary procedures used in his occupation to deal with incompetency. Hence, these may be necessary to ensure high standards in practitioners who have not the ethic of the professional ideology. Even so, altruism may not appear very rational unless human life has meaning or purpose. Whether they benefit directly or indirectly from the service, to serve clients because of their humanity is to move towards the position advocated by Schumacher, even though it does not necessarily take on the overtly religious perspective that he proposed. Whether value is imparted to human life because of the existence of a creator, as Schumacher implies, or whether it is taken as 'a priori', is not the concern of this chapter.

Nevertheless, this is an essential element in any discussion about why a professional must be competent: either because the individual accepts that this is the demand of the profession, or the demand of his professionalism, or his professionalism is a result of his metaphysical or religious beliefs. In the last instance there are implications that the professional is a person of a particular disposition, belief or ideology. Disposition and belief are individualistic and it may be wrong or immoral for professions to expect conformity in either disposition or religious belief. However, it may also be immoral for a profession to retain within its ranks practitioners whose attitudes towards their occupation (ideology) do not result in competent professional practice. Hence, if at the heart of professionalism lies a desire for competency in order to benefit the client, then the initial self-evident assumption appears to be justified.

But it might be argued that if it is necessary for the practitioner to conform to the ideology of competency for the sake of service to the client, then by what criteria is this attitude measured during training? Indeed:

Has any professional school and professional faculty ever said to a student, 'You cannot go on to this particular school because you are not qualified, not in terms of your intellect, not in terms of your proficiency, but because you are not the kind of person we want in this profession?' (Ver Steeg in Boley 1977: 90)

Or perhaps, more significantly, do professional schools pass or fail students because their attitudes and/or ideologies do/do not conform to those laid down in the training curriculum? Alternatively, it may be wondered how attitudes are assessed since a number of professional bodies, e.g. the Panel of Assessors for District Nurse Training, specify them in their curriculum. This may occur on an informal basis during training in practical placement and in the professional school. Yet if the 'correct' attitudes are not exhibited, should the training programme include deliberate attempts by the tutors to mould the students' attitudes towards the practice of the job? If this process is embarked upon, then it must be recognised that the nature of the training programme may have ceased to be an educational process and become one of training or even indoctrination. Since this point will be referred to again later, it will not be pursued here.

At this juncture it must be recognised that the educator in the professions might never have undertaken this type of analysis since, on another level, his task is to prepare students for entry into the profession and so long as the majority of them appear competent to the profession in the qualifying exam-

inations, then his task has been achieved. Initially, this argument might appear sufficient since it restricts the aims of the
education process to education itself, but it reduces the end-
product to the successful negotiation of examination hurdles.
This then might also equate the educational process with instruction and training, an equation that will be discussed later.
However, it says little about why the practitioner should be competent, except that he should be competent enough in order to
pass the qualifying examinations. But does this actually demonstrate that he has been prepared for his work? Possibly not, so
that it is suggested that Schumacher's approach has a great
deal to commend it, for he writes:

'How do we prepare young people for the future world of
work?' And the first answer, I think must be: we should
prepare them to be able to distinguish between good work and
bad work and encourage them not to accept the latter.
(1977: 61)

This raises issues about the content of the curriculum in the
education of professionals and, also, about the method of teaching students: points to which reference will be made elsewhere.
Nevertheless, Schumacher's argument implies that one of the
aims of professional education should be to produce recruits to
the profession who are aware of the standards of competency
and who are not prepared to accept or practise anything below
what they regard as good and competent. This then is a moral
issue that lies at the very heart of professionalism itself and,
therefore, at the centre of the education of professionals. But
the issue of competency is itself difficult and complex, so that
it is now necessary to examine the second query raised about
this self-evident assertion of the aim of professional education.

What is Competency?

At the outset of this discussion it is assumed that competency
is only achieved when the occupation is performed proficiently
in all of its aspects, i.e. good practice based upon sound
theory. This demands that the practitioner should have both
the knowledge and the skill to undertake the demands of the
job, proficiency in one but not the other area is less than competency. Neither knowledge or skill, however, are self-evident
concepts when applied to professional practice.
Professional knowledge may refer to the mastery of the
academic discipline, or disciplines, that underlie the professional
practice. It is maintained here that mastery of this knowledge is
essential to the concept of professionalism, a point to which
further reference will be made below. In addition to this
academic knowledge, it is essential for the practitioner to understand the theoretical basis to the skills involved in the performance of professional practice. Yet few occupations are performed

'in vacuo', so that knowledge of how to relate to members of the role-set of professional practice is also important. One final area of knowledge necessary for the professional is that of the moral values necessary to undertake professional practice. By contrast, skills are about performing the occupation rather than about the theory. Performance of these skills may be dependent upon knowledge but, for the sake of clarity, the two are discussed separately here. Hence skills may refer to the sheer ability to perform certain techniques or procedures acceptable to the professional or prescribed by the organisations employing professionals. Additionally, social skills by which individual practitioners interrelate with their role-set are essential to the performance of the occupation. Competence, therefore, is a far broader concept than initially implied in the opening discussion of this chapter - it relates to knowledge, skills and attitudes. 'Attitudes' are included within this analysis and relate to the professional ideology mentioned above: they have cognitive and affective dimensions and also a behavioural tendency. It is now possible to summarise this discussion in the Table 3.1, indicating the elements of professional competency. Thus, it may be seen that the foundations of professional practice are far more complex and that competency to practise is much broader than often assumed and, if Schumacher is right, then the attitudinal dimension is more important than it often appears to be in professional training. Indeed, it might be possible to rephrase Ver Steeg's question and ask whether individuals are debarred from entering practice because they do not have the 'right attitudes'. Should professional practitioners be debarred from practice if they do not have the right attitude? At this stage it might be sufficient to claim that since professionalism is ideological, failure to exhibit a professional attitude towards competency, in all of its aspects, might be sufficient grounds for suspension from practice.

Table 3.1 The Elements of Professional Competency

Knowledge and Understanding of:	Skills to:	Professional Attitudes
-Academic discipline(s) -The psycho-motor elements -Interpersonal relationships -Moral values	-Perform psycho-motor procedures -Interact with others	Knowledge of professionalism Emotive commitment to professionalism Willingness to perform professionally

Attitudes might be relatively slow to change, especially if they have been internalised and become a part of the ego-identity of the practitioner. By contrast, technical knowledge and skills are not static, neither are they likely to be. Hence competency

is not static either. The ideology of professionalism, which
demands that the practitioner keeps abreast with recent developments in his field, may be sufficient stimulus for him to keep on
learning in order to remain competent. Yet it is possible for
practitioners to fail to keep abreast. Berg (1973: 108) has claimed
that there are 'doubts about whether the benefits that managers
apparently believe accompany educational credentials do in fact
materialize'. Indeed, Rogers (1962) showed that 16 per cent of
the general medical practitioners surveyed in an American research project were slow to adopt an innovation – these he
called laggards. Laggards were further removed from the source
of developments than were earlier adopters and they also relied
more upon their peers for information than they did for obtaining
this from professional journals and conferences. It might be
argued that rapid adoption of new ideas is not always good but
Rogers showed that those who adopt or reject an innovation
early in the cycle of diffusion spend longer testing it than do
the laggards, so that they tend not to be irresponsible. Hence
if the laggard medical practitioners fail to adopt a life-saving
drug for two years, their patients are put at risk for the whole
of that period, so that the failure to keep abreast with developments may be regarded as immoral. Additionally, it might be
claimed that if these practitioners had the correct attitude
towards continued learning these situations would never occur.
This example might be regarded as an extreme one, nevertheless the principle remains the same – that it may be immoral for
anyone who is viewed by other people as professional to practise
if his knowledge is deficient and that the right attitude towards
professional practice is essential to competency in a rapidly
changing world.

Clearly, as professional knowledge expands and fragments, the
profession itself will develop specialist branches and no new
recruit can be prepared for all of these nor can competency in
any of them be expected at the outset. Therefore, as specialities
develop the question needs to be raised about precisely what
specialism the recruits are being prepared for and whether they
have the right attitude for it. Thus it may be argued that no
new entrant to a profession may be trained to be competent to
practise in a specialised branch of the profession but only to
have the foundations upon which competency in practice can be
built. Nevertheless, some form of competency or minimum
standards during and at the termination of initial training may
have to be achieved, although Berg (1973) does suggest that
there is little evidence to relate standards achieved in professional training to success in practice. Therefore, if no such
evidence exists, why should there be terminal examinations or
other forms of assessment during training? Is it to ensure
standards are maintained? This could be the case but it is not
known how proficient those who failed in training would have
been had they been allowed to practice. Yet many who fail one
or more hurdle do eventually complete the course and practise

successfully, so that some evidence exists to indicate that failure at any hurdle may not preclude successful practice. Examinations and other assessment procedures may not test competency but merely motivate the recruit to learn and internalise theory and practice. There may be other reasons for assessment procedures but at least some doubt must exist as to whether they actually test competency to practise in the profession.

Competency has been employed throughout this discussion, although no attempt has been made to define it. Professions vary in the ways that they seek to assess competency. Some, such as accountancy, law and nursing, have national examinations whereas others, such as health visiting and some engineering professions, accept a local educational institution's own assessment procedures. Nearly all professions validate the courses for training, having their own requirements about what should be taught but not all actually undertake the assessment procedures nationally. Even in centralised examination procedures, variation of standards is known to occur and in localised systems this must also be present. Therefore, competency to enter the profession does not depend on having reached an objective standard in all of the facets specified in Table 3.1, but rather on the successful negotiation of whatever system of qualifying examinations that a profession or professional school implements. The level of ability, as measured by these tests, which is considered to be an acceptable standard of competency is almost certain to vary from one training establishment to another and none may relate to the level of competency exhibited in practice thereafter. Hence, it would be unwise to attempt to define the concept of competency in objective terms, although it may be that within a profession competency is viewed as a level of professional practice which provides service appropriate to the wants/needs and expectations of the clients.

Competency to practise is not, therefore, an objective nor static standard. It is not even guaranteed by success in the qualifying examinations, so that it is maintained here that competency to practise is not the logical aim of professional training. It may be questioned whether the professional school actually has any responsibility for the standards of practice in the profession at all or whether it should limit its aims to the training process itself. If the latter argument is supported, then two alternative sets of aims appear logical at this stage in the discussion; either the professional school should seek to produce new recruits to the profession who, at the completion of their training, have a sufficient level of knowledge and skills to enter practice and the profession will ensure thereafter that its standards are maintained; or, it should produce new recruits to the profession who have a sufficient level of knowledge and skills to enter practice and a professional ideology of seeking to ensure the maintenance of good practice. Clearly these alternatives have implications for the curriculum: if the former is adopted it is possible to have a course directly related to professional practice, whereas, if the latter one is, then more of the course might be devoted to moulding 'right' attitudes. However, this latter approach raises questions about the educational process itself which requires discussion.

THE EDUCATIONAL PROCESS

Peters (1967: 14) has suggested that the educational process 'can be viewed as a family of tasks leading up to the achievement of being educated'. Nowhere does he suggest that one of these tasks in education is indoctrination, yet the implications of indoctrination are present in the second aim suggested above and in the references to Schumacher's work. Indoctrination as a process will be discussed in the chapter considering the philosophy of educational processes so that its ramifications will not be dwelt upon here. Even so, it is important to recognise that the debate about indoctrination covers consideration of aims, content and methods of teaching and learning. Since this chapter is about the aims of professional education, it is necessary to consider indoctrination from this perspective. Hare (1964) has argued that in order to understand the concept of indoctrination it is initially necessary to view it from the perspective of aims. He suggests that in indoctrination the aim is to produce in the recipient those views that the indoctrinator wishes to purvey, whilst the educator is concerned to help the student hold values which reflect considered and reasoned argument. He goes on to suggest that in initial education 'the educator is trying to turn the children into adults; the indoctrinator is trying to make them perpetual children' (1964: 64). Whilst the values implicit in the terms 'adult' and 'children' are debatable, the idea that Hare is expounding is much more acceptable. Indoctrination might, therefore, occur in professional training although this is not its aim. To seek always to master new knowledge and skills in order to serve the client or patient because he has been taught to, or because of the fear of consequences of professional malpractice, is hardly sufficient reason for professional practice. At the heart of the professional ideology lies an acceptance of its values which has resulted from a sustained educational process during which students have been encouraged to make a critical appraisal of the ethics of professionalism. During this process the student will have had opportunity to withdraw from training if he or she has been unable to subscribe to its values or is unwilling to accept its demands. This, therefore, has implications for the curriculum of professional training since the inclusion of the study of professionalism, professional ethics and, therefore, interpersonal relationships becomes more significant. But it is an educational process, not indoctrination. Hence it may be necessary to expand Peters' (1967: 14) conception of the achievement of being educated for the professional, from 'the mastery of some skills, knowledge and understanding of principles' to the mastery of some skills, knowledge and the

understanding of principles and an understanding and acceptance
of the values underlying the practice of those skills and that
knowledge within a profession.

At this stage in the discussion it is now possible to return to
the two sets of aims for professional education suggested at the
end of the previous section, namely:

(a)   the professional school should aim to produce new recruits
       to the profession who, at the completion of their training,
       have a sufficient level of knowledge and skills to enter
       practice and the profession will ensure thereafter that
       its standards are maintained, or

(b)   the professional school should aim to produce new recruits
       to the profession who have a professional ideology of
       seeking to ensure good practice as well as a sufficient
       level of knowledge and skills to enter practice.

Since it has been claimed that it is possible to help students
acquire a professional ideology without indoctrination this should
be among the main aims of professional education, because it
should mean that as practitioners the students will be committed
to standards of excellence that will lead them to keep abreast
with developments in their profession. It is also maintained here
that while it is possible, it is logically inconsistent to train people
to enter the professions who do not subscribe to a high view
of professional practice. The inconsistency lies in the fact that
professionalism demands that the practitioner should be the
master of the knowledge and skills necessary to his practice
whenever he practises, and to run the risk of producing laggards
as a result of training is to give professional accreditation to
individuals who may not perform professionally after a period in
practice.

Nevertheless, the education of professionals does not occur
'in vacuo' so that it is now necessary to examine the aims of
this aspect of education in relation to the society and the
profession.

THE EDUCATION OF PROFESSIONALS AND THE NEEDS OF
SOCIETY

Holloman (1977: 19), apropos of engineering education, implies
that the aims should be related to the needs of the wider
society. This claim raises two quite separate, but significant,
issues within any discussion of the aims of professional education:
these being the place of education in society and the concept of
needs.

Needs is a concept used frequently in education and it will be
discussed in detail later in this chapter. Even so, it is important
to enquire whether society actually has needs and, if it does,
the relation of education to them. As an abstract concept society

cannot experience any form of need but, in order to survive, individual social systems may have a number of requisites that ensure smooth functioning. The American sociologist, Talcott Parsons, in a number of works, discusses the necessary pre-requisites for a social system to survive and he suggests that there are four: integration, pattern maintenance, goal attainment and adaptation (1971: 4ff). Parsons has been criticised by sociologists because of the built-in conservatism of his analysis but if a social system has prerequisites in order to survive he may have isolated some of them. It could then be argued that the initial education institution has served to ensure some form of integration and pattern maintenance in society by transmitting the accepted cultural values of one generation to the next. Indeed this function of education is reflected in John Stuart Mill's (cited in Lester-Smith 1966: 9) claim that the heart of education lies in 'the culture which each generation purposely gives to those who are to be their successors'. While it has already been argued that education need not necessarily reflect an inter-generational perspective, it is clear from many sociological studies of initial education that the transmission of accepted culture, usually that of the established elite, is one of its major functions. Nevertheless, the functions of an institution are not synonymous with its aims and few educationalists today would claim that the aim of education is to transmit the established culture to the next generation.

Similarly, it might be argued that the professions serve to ensure the smooth functioning of the social system and are, therefore, an element in the prerequisites of the social system. While many might not want to question this analysis of the functions of a profession, educationalists should seek to distinguish this from professional education. Indeed, the aims of professional education and the functions of the profession are distinct. It is, therefore, claimed here, that there is no intrinsic connection between the needs of society and the aims of professional education. It is now necessary, therefore, to explore the relationship between the needs of the profession and its educational system.

THE EDUCATION OF PROFESSIONALS, THE NEEDS OF THE PROFESSION AND THE DEMANDS OF PRACTICE

Earlier it was suggested that one of the main aims of professional education should be to produce recruits to the profession having a professional attitude towards practice as well as sufficient knowledge and skill to enter the profession in order to become a practitioner. The demands of practice may, however, result in the new recruit to the profession endeavouring to learn new knowledge and skills so that he can continue to respond to the demands of efficient practice. In response to these demands professional education may offer an ongoing programme known by a variety of terms, e.g. in-service, post-basic, continuing

education. This might appear to relegate professional education,
in an institutional sense, to being the handmaiden of the profession. However, it is suggested here that this view of
professional education is functional in the sense suggested in
the above analyses.

In the same way it would be possible to argue that even if the
needs of a professional could be isolated, professional education
would only be seen to be a functional part of the professional
system in the manner in which it responded to them and, therefore, this would not provide the aims for professional education.

The perspective of placing the education of professionals into
the wider professional and social systems may not be unrealistic
but it may distort an analysis of the aims of professional education by trying to locate these beyond the institutional education
process. If this were undertaken, it would allow the process to
be evaluated in terms of its effect on the system. This is the
classical formulation of utilitarianism: the good or bad act is
evaluated in terms of its consequences. Such an argument is
open to all the objections of the utilitarian position including
relegating 'good' education to that which responds to the
requirements of the system rather than that which produces
something in the learners. MacIntyre (1964: 2) suggests that
the 'reason why utilitarianism dominates us is that it provides
us with our only public criterion for securing agreement on
moral and political questions' so that it is hardly surprising that
educational institutions fall victim to it. He points out:

> The means-end picture is read in contemporary terms as one in
> which production is the means, consumption the end. So real
> human satisfaction belongs to consumption. The criterion of pro-
> duction is efficiency, for production is only a means. (1964: 7)

Yet education is not a means to an end, as Dewey (1916: 50)
clearly specifies: 'the educational process has no end beyond
itself; it is its own end . . . This is in accord with MacIntyre's
(1964: 19) conclusion that the key to educational theory lies in
an aim that ought 'to help people to discover activities whose
ends are not outside themselves; and it happens to be of all
intellectual inquiry that in and for itself it provides just such
activity'. This conclusion relates to the earlier argument that
the aims of professional education should be to provide an
opportunity for recruits to the profession to gain an awareness
of good practice and a determination to shun less than the best,
plus preparing the entrant with the necessary knowledge and
skill to embark upon his career. Thus the aims of the educational
process are about the learners rather than about the profession
or the wider society. This is not to deny that there is not a
connection between training and practice, only to assert that
the aims of professional education may not relate intrinsically
to the needs of the profession nor to those of the wider society.

THE LEARNER AND THE EDUCATION OF PROFESSIONALS

Dewey (1916: 51) has argued that:

> Since life means growth, a living creature lives as truly and
> positively at one stage as at another, with the same intrinsic
> fullness and the same absolute claims. Hence education means
> the enterprise of supplying the conditions which insure growth,
> or adequacy of life, irrespective of age.

While Dewey may be a little too all-embracing in the claims he
makes for education, it is clear that for him education must have
a humanistic base.

Development must occur through the process. This condition
has more recently been re-echoed by William Taylor (1980: 336ff)
who has argued that professional development of school teachers
should result in personal growth. Yet this conclusion may be
open to the same objections as were raised about education being
utilitarian. Personal growth may be achieved by means other
than education, so that it lies beyond the educational process:
it may not be the aim of education, nor of professional education
in particular.

Yet, since the learner is involved in the process it is impossible
to see the aims without some reference to the learner himself.
Indeed, earlier, it was argued that the main aim of professional
education is to produce attitudes, knowledge and skills in the
learner. But this is a particular type of end-product, one that
is intrinsically connected with the educational process per se, so
that it may be that this particular type of growth and development in the learner may be a legitimate aim for education –
provided that growth and development are viewed in terms of
attitudes, knowledge and skills and in the case of professional
education, relating to the profession.

Education cannot be said to have occurred unless the learner
has learned and understood something, in this instance about
the professional attitudes and knowledge and skills essential to
embark upon a professional career. Yet merely to acquire
attitudes, knowledge and skills may not indicate that the learner
has been educated, as opposed to trained, instructed, etc. He
may not have developed or grown as an individual, nor may he
have gained the critical faculties necessary to enable him to
decide what is good practice, what is significant knowledge or
what are relevant skills. Hence it is suggested here that acquiring the art of assessing, judging what is best, etc. in any
circumstances may be an element of education. MacIntyre (1964:
19) claims that the 'critical ability which ought to be the fruit
of education serves nothing directly except for itself, no one
except those who exercise it'.

Personal development may be varied in the acquisition of the
ability to be critically aware and assess what is good or bad
practice and, in this sense, the aims of professional education

may relate to personal development in the learner. MacIntyre goes on to argue that since critical standards claim social recognition they demand a democratic community in which they can be exercised. This democratic community, in this instance, may be the profession, the community of peers with specialised attitudes, knowledge and skills, in which the professional may exercise those critical standards that are the result of his education, both in the profession and beyond it.

At this stage, it may be useful to recapitulate the tenor of the argument thus far in the chapter. It has been claimed that the aims of any form of education must not lie beyond the process, since those which do are of a utilitarian nature and therefore invalid. Hence competency to practise is not a legitimate aim in professional education. Rather, producing in the learner the ability to recognise good practice and the determination to ensure that his own future practice will not fall below this standard is a major aim. Additionally, it is claimed that since knowledge and skills change rapidly an aim of education is not to provide knowledge and skills sufficient for good practice, so much as to provide the learner with sufficient knowledge and skills for him to enter the profession and to embark upon his career. Finally, it is claimed that an aim of professional education is not professional development per se but increasing the learner's critical awareness so that he develops in those aspects of his life that relate to the professional practice and which are relevant to lifelong learning.

Having reached this stage in the argument, it is recognised that society's needs and the profession's needs and the learner's needs, wants and interests have not been fully discussed, so that it is now necessary to enquire into the relationship between these and the aims of professional education.

THE EDUCATION OF PROFESSIONALS AND NEEDS, WANTS AND INTERESTS

Hirst and Peters (1970: 33) suggest that a whole book could be written solely around the emphasis placed upon needs and interests so that to raise this issue at this stage in the chapter may appear to be inappropriate. Nevertheless, it is intended to discuss only some of those points relevant to the aims of the education of professionals. Clearly, any form of needs, wants or interests unrelated to the educational process per se may not constitute a relevant discussion since they will almost certainly relate either to the functions of the educational process or to the motivation for instituting the process. Hence, this discussion will be restricted to those needs, wants and interests that are intrinsic to the process: these, it may be argued, must therefore relate to either teachers or learners. However, it was shown earlier that the teachers are not essential to the educational process either, even those who may have planned and developed the curriculum, so that their needs, wants and interests are only coincidental to the process. The only

person who is essential to the process is the learner, so that no
other kind of needs, wants or interests are considered here.
These are dealt with in reverse order, so that interests are
discussed first.

Interests

Like all of these terms 'interests' is both a complex and ambigious
one. It may, for instance, relate to the professional well-being
of the student, or to the interest that the student shows in a
particular aspect of the course. Clearly the teacher seeks to
design a course with the professional well-being of his students
in mind. Nevertheless, it would be quite false to claim that the
aim of professional education is to secure the professional well-
being of the student: this may, however, be a function of a
successful course or a particular professional school. It may
occur because certain teachers, schools or students are well-
connected in the profession but it is not the aim of professional
education. Indeed, since it was argued earlier that an aspect
of professionalism is the service ethic, it might be logically
inconsistent to argue that an aim of professional education is
both to produce practitioners with this and ones who at the
same time seek to preserve their self-interest.

Interests may also relate to motivation. In one sense it has
been claimed that an aim of professional education is to produce
practitioners who are motivated to act professionally. However,
if an aim of professional education is to motivate students to be
interested in the subjects that they have to learn then it may
be claimed either that the selection process was erroneous and
the wrong students have been admitted to the course, or that
the teaching and learning process has resulted in demotivating
students. If this is the case, then there could be a number of
reasons for this occurring, including the fact that the students
do not see the relevance of what they are studying for their
future occupational practice or that the teaching-learning process is itself uninteresting. In either case, this is a matter of
concern for the criteria of selection of curriculum content or
for the methods of presenting the material rather than of the
aims of education itself. Additionally, the creation of interest
may be a legitimate objective of a lesson or a series of lessons,
but this is to distinguish clearly between objectives for specific
sessions and the overall aims of the education of professionals.
It is, therefore, claimed here that there is no intrinsic connection between interests and the aims of professional education.

Wants

This term is rather similar to interests within the context of
professional education. Since the learner wants to become a
professional practitioner he has embarked upon a specific educational process. So long as the learner's wants are in accord

with the aims of the process of education he is undergoing there should be an ongoing process of learning. However, it may not be a function, and it is certainly not an aim of, education to create wants in the student. Even so, it is recognised that if the process has been successful the learner might be stimulated to learn even more and in this sense motivation may be regarded as a function of professional education, but not as one of its aims.

However, there is one point at which the wants of the learner approximate to the aims of education and this is in professional practice: recognition that a practitioner has not been able to serve his clients as efficiently as he desires may generate a want to embark upon another educational programme that will provide him with even more knowledge and skill. This want is akin to the aim of professional education but it still relates to the motivation of the learner and the two only coincide where the learner actually designs his own learning programme. Then the aim of the educational process will coincide with the motivation for undertaking it - to respond to a professionally induced want. It is at this point that there is great similarity between the aims of education and the needs of the student, to which reference will be made during the next sub-section.

Needs

In everyday speech the term 'need' is employed with a variety of meanings, each conveyed through the linguistic structure and the social context in which it is employed. Sometimes it is used synonymously with 'wants', as is evident from the previous sub-section, and often it relates to the fulfilment of interests. Additionally, the term frequently incorporates implications of 'moral ought' within its usage. Perhaps this failure to use the term rigorously in common speech is one reason why its elaboration has been so restricted in the philosophy of education and another reason may be the complexity of its use in other disciplines.

Hirst and Peters (1970: 33) suggest that there are needs of a diagnostic, biological, physiological, basic and functional type, whereas Bradshaw (1977) considers that there are normative, felt, expressed and comparative needs. Additionally, Maslow (1954) discussed physiological, safety, social, self-esteem and self-fulfilment needs and Halmos (1978) distinguished between primary and secondary ones. Such is the profusion of prefixes to the term 'need' that it is hardly surprising that it is frequently employed but rarely defined. In biology, however, it refers to an imbalance in the body tissues which results in the body organisms being energised to rectify either the deficit or the excess. In Bradshaw's work in social welfare, the term relates more to the deficit than it does to the excess, and it is this deficit that Lawson has utilised in his definition of an educational need. Lawson (1975: 37) has suggested that where 'a deficiency can be remedied by the help of some educational process' then an educational need has been established. Such a definition raises problems about the definition of and the relative nature of 'deficiency' as well as methodological problems about discovering such a condition. Lawson, himself, rightly raises some of these issues in his philosophical studies of adult education.

Yet it will be seen that Lawson's idea that an educational need is a deficiency may also relate closely to Bradshaw's 'felt needs' and 'expressed needs' and to the earlier discussion in this chapter on 'wants'. Perhaps the term 'need' carries with it other connotations that explains why it is such a popular term in education. Some of these, such as the needs of society and of the profession, have already been discussed here and it is suggested that education may be viewed in a functional manner and analysed from this perspective but that to regard an aim of education in such a utilitarian manner is to confuse aims and functions. Another reason for its popularity may be because of the overtones of absoluteness and necessity that it carries. Indeed, Wiltshire (1973) clearly suggested that the utilisation of the term in adult education was to distract educators from the purpose of education and he wrote (1976: 146) that the term drives 'a gap between thinking and practice' so that educators concentrate their attention upon techniques rather than upon purposes.

Clearly this discussion is tending to suggest that 'needs' are not so significant to the consideration of the aims of education as they have frequently been assumed to be. Lawson warns about the use of the term when he suggests that to define the aims of education in non-educational terms runs the risk of having education defined as social work, community development, etc. Hirst and Peters also recognise terms even though they recognise that the satisfaction of specific needs may be a necessary condition for learning.

Wiltshire discussed the concept of learning need rather than educational need. The professional recognises, as a result of his professionalism, that he is deficient in specific aspects of knowledge and skill necessary to practise professionally. He has a felt and recognised learning need, a 'want', in terms of the earlier discussion, and recognises the need for additional, specific education – which he can design for himself or for which he can undertake additional courses. If he does either of these, then his motivation to learn has stemmed from his recognised deficiency. It is then possible to define the aims of that educational process in terms of his need.

It was suggested, initially, that the aims of the educational process involved attitudes towards good practice, knowledge and skills sufficient to enter the profession and also to increase the learner's critical awareness. In the instance of continuing education (in-service, post-basic, etc.), the provision of 'knowledge and skill sufficient to enter the profession' may be

rephrased as 'knowledge and skills sufficient to enhance the
learner's ability to practise professionally'. In this instance, the
aims of education approximate to the learner's motivation but it
is still maintained that it is logically incorrect to confuse the
aims of the educational process with the motivation of the learner.
However, it would be possible at this stage to argue that the
aims of a specific educational process may be specified legitimately
in the terms of the perceived learning needs of a professional
practitioner, i.e. the aim of a course in continuing education is
to provide professional practitioners with the opportunity to
satisfy the learning needs perceived from within their professional
practice. Yet in the case of the laggards, mentioned earlier,
their perception of their own learning needs might be totally
different from those that their more aware colleagues stipulated
for them. Thus the professionally aware may be in a position to
perceive their learning needs in terms of the knowledge there
is to know and the skills that there are to be learned but other
practitioners may be less able to do this. Hence, if this were the
only aim of an educational process it would appear to be inconsistent with the aim of providing opportunity to gain the knowledge and skill sufficient to enhance the learning ability to
practise professionally, so that the perceived learning needs
may only be a legitimate aim for any form of professional education when it is consistent with these wider aims. It is perhaps
more likely that the perceived learning needs of the professional
practitioner may form one of the criteria for the selection of
curriculum content and become one of the objectives of a
specific course rather than forming a basis for specifying the
aim of any element of professional education.

Additionally, it might be argued that in the more hierarchically
structured professions, a superior's perceptions of the
deficiencies in the professional practice of a junior may be
sufficient reason for sending him on an additional course. Nevertheless, the superior's perception of the needs of the practitioner
provide the rationale for sending him on a course rather than
the actual aims of the course itself and the satisfaction of the
practitioner's specific deficiencies may form one of the criteria
for the selection of the content.

Thus, it may be wondered whether there is any basis in the
often drawn equation between the aims of education and the needs
of the learners. It appears that many of the reasons why this
linkage is often drawn reside in a confusion between the aims
of the providers of the educational process and the motivation
of the learners. Yet in the case of continuing education there
may be more substance than this: deficiency occurs in the
standards of professional practice either because the practitioner
does not have the motivation to keep abreast with professional
developments or for some other reason, so that a need exists.
Specific courses are mounted to rectify this deficiency and in
this instance an aim of the course may be to satisfy a professional
need that some practitioners have experienced. Such a course

may be of a limited duration, say 3-4 weeks, and in this instance there appears to be almost a legitimate equation between professional need and the aim of the course. Yet this appears to run counter to the argument that education should not have utilitarian aims; not that aims and actions should not be confused. This problem may be resolved in the following manner.

If the aim of the course is to teach the practitioners a specific skill and its associated knowledge then it may be questioned whether the aim is actually educational or something less, i.e. training. If it is educational and specific, then it might be approximating towards educational objectives for a specific short course rather than providing an overall aim for professional continuing education. If, however, the aim of professional continuing education is to continue to provide opportunity for the practitioners to enhance their knowledge, skill and professional awareness, then the response to specific perceived needs may be viewed within this wider context and the objectives of specific courses may be more narrow than this overall aim. Hence, in this instance, needs may relate to objectives of specific courses rather than the aims of education in general.

CONCLUSION

This chapter opened with the suggestion that the aim of professional education is self-evident: to produce a competent practitioner. Such an assertion was not denied, it was merely suggested that the term meant very little. After much discussion it has been concluded that the aims of professional education should be more meaningful and realistic. First, the process should produce recruits to the profession that have a professional ideology, especially in relation to understanding good practice and service. Secondly, that the educational process should provide the new recruit with sufficient knowledge and skills, or the continuing practitioners with enhanced knowledge and skills, to enter, or to continue in, the profession. Finally, that the process should result in the practitioner developing an increased sense of critical awareness.

Needs, wants and interests have been discussed, and it has been suggested that the prevalence of these terms in education has been because two sets of confusions have arisen: first between the aims and functions of education and, secondly, between the aims of education and the motivation of the learners. Both the functions of education and the motivation of the learners provide reasons for the educational process but in neither case are they educational reasons per se, so that it was not considered legitimate to view them as educational aims.

Perhaps the argument of this chapter is best summarised by a quotation from Houle (1980: 75):

The ultimate aim of every advanced, subtle and mature form of continuing education is to convey a complex attitude made up of a readiness to use the best ideas and techniques of the moment but also to expect that they will be modified or replaced. The new machine will soon be antiquated, the new drug will be outmoded, the new principle will yield to a more profound one, and the revolutionary approach will become first familiar and then old fashioned. Everyone must expect constant change and with it new goals to be achieved and new understanding and skill to be mastered.

Attitudes, knowledge and skill and a critical awareness to test, try, change and modify so that the professional may be abreast of all developments in order to serve his client because less than the best is a denial of both the meaning of professionalism and, more ultimately, the meaning of humanity itself.

4 CRITERIA FOR THE SELECTION OF CURRICULUM CONTENT IN PROFESSIONAL EDUCATION

In the previous chapter the aims of professional education were elaborated and, clearly, if they are to be achieved, it is necessary that the content of what is to be taught or learned must be in accord with them. However, these aims do not constitute the only reason why specific content is included within the curriculum, and the purpose of this chapter is to explore the underlying rationale for determining that certain knowledge, skills and attitudes should be acquired during the process of professional education or professional continuing education.

At the outset of this discussion, it is necessary to draw a distinction between what the designers of the curriculum, or the syllabus, intend the learning outcomes to be and, therefore, included in a written curricula, syllabus or programme and what is actually taught and learned in the process of education itself. Reasons for the inclusion of content in the curriculum or syllabus constitute one element in the discussion but, once these have been stipulated or agreed between the professional body and the educational institution, then the stipulation or agreement itself constitutes another set of criteria why the specific content is included in the educational process. In order to attempt to simplify this, the remainder of the chapter is divided into two parts, the first dealing with the specific content in the curriculum and the second focusing upon the actual educational process itself.

THE INTENTION TO INCLUDE SPECIFIC CONTENT IN THE CURRICULUM

Curricula for professional education are constructed either by the professional body itself, in which case there is usually a specified minimum syllabus or an examination syllabus, or by the staff of the academic institution who are teaching the course. In the latter instance, the curriculum that they design is usually submitted for approval to the appropriate internal committees of the educational establishment and, for validation as approval, to the professional body. When a course is offered in a polytechnic or an institution of higher education in the United Kingdom, there is often a second validating body involved, e.g. the Council for National Academic Awards. However, in the case of courses taught in universities having a Royal Charter, the university is empowered to award its own certificate, diploma or degree. In some professions, such as architecture, the professional courses are taught in both universities and polytechnics, so that the students gain their professional recognition and the appropriate award of a university or the CNAA. Nevertheless, it is not the intention to review procedures for the validation of professional educational courses here, but rather to examine the reasons why certain content is included in the curriculum or syllabus constructed. Two major factors may be isolated here which constitute the basis for further discussion: the aims of professional education and the perceived demands of professional practice.

The Aims of Professional Education

The distinction between 'aims' and 'objectives' has not been elaborated in this study since it is hardly pertinent to the issues under discussion. However, at the outset of the previous chapter, mention was made of the fact that aims tend to be broad, philosophical statements of intent in the educational process, whereas objectives are more frequently stated in relation to specific teaching and learning situations. However, there is some diversity of usages of these terms among different curriculum theorists, although this will not be discussed here. Suffice to note that 'aims' are treated as broad philosophical statements of interest, whilst 'objectives' are regarded as intended teaching or learning outcomes of specific parts of the educational process. Both are clearly related to that aspect of education specified in the definition formulated earlier – 'any planned series of incidents directed towards . . .' In the sense of planning, they are both intrinsic to the educational process. However, since objectives are usually regarded as only relating to one part of the curriculum, they must be seen to be dependent upon the aims of the educational process, rather than formulations that are independent and freestanding. It is, therefore, important to examine the aims of professional education formulated in the previous chapter in relation to this present discussion.

It was claimed, for instance, that the learner's acquisition of a professional ideology is a significant aim of professional education: that ideology is about the desire to continue to learn in order to be the master of the professional knowledge upon which the practice is founded, so that the practitioner can render the best service to his clients. If this is not to occur as a result of indoctrination or socialisation, but rather through an educational process, it is important that certain disciplines are included in the professional curriculum that relate to this. A number of disciplines appear most important within this context including ethics applied to the specific profession, e.g. medical ethics, engineering ethics. Yet Holloman (1977: 19ff), who devotes a considerable part of his paper to ethics in engineering, does not think that there is much difference between

the lay person and the professional engineer except, so he
claims, 'the engineer . . . is a knowledgeable professional . . .
(who) has a particular responsibility to inform the rest of us of
the consequences to society of actions with respect to technological
matters' (1977: 24). The implications in his statement are that
these are self-evident matters for the engineer and, yet, it may
be that they are more complex than he suggests, so that the
study of engineering ethics would at least provide an academic
basis upon which the engineer might consider these matters.
But applied ethics may only be the start of this process since
Pellegrino (1977: 12) wishes to extend this and calls for the
'exchange between medicine and the humanities' to be deepened.
Clearly, he is recognising that in medicine the professional is
more than one who merely goes through the motions of doctoring
and that his education should be broader and include various
forms of knowledge. Within this context, it may be that
'professionalism' as employed here, may itself constitute the
basis of a course of study during initial education and training,
so that those who are about to enter a professional occupation
may study and exhibit those qualities of person that might
typify a professional.

It will be recalled that the second aim of professional education
specified earlier was that sufficient knowledge and skill should
be gained so that the new recruit to the profession is competent
to enter professional practice. Clearly, this statement calls into
question the concept of knowledge itself, which will be discussed
in the next chapter. Even so, the facets of knowledge and skill
that constitute a foundation upon which competency can be constructed have already been discussed. Hence, this provides a
rationale for inclusion within the curriculum of a wide range of
theory and practice relevant to the specific professional practice.
It is interesting to note that theory is regarded as more important
than practice, in many instances, so that so-called sandwich
courses are sometimes regarded by some as being less academic
than courses that are totally of a theoretical nature. Indeed in
some professions, such as the clergy, there has been a tendency
to leave most practical training until after the completion of the
academic course. There is an implied value in this practice; that
the theory is more important than the practice. This value is
prevalent throughout British society and is one that will be
examined within the context of professional education later in this
study. Without anticipating that discussion, it must be pointed
out that the theoretician who has few skills may be unable to use
his professional knowledge for the benefit of anyone, even himself,
and this appears to lessen the value of the acquisition of knowledge
itself. Hence, it is suggested that as both theory and practice are
intrinsic and complementary parts of professional practice they
should also occur in the educational process, although whether
this should be by a sandwich or by practical placement as a
recurrent feature of the whole course is a matter for professions
to decide in the light of the demands of their practice.

The final aim of professional education specified in the previous chapter was that of critical awareness, a state that was implicit in the word 'understanding' in the definition formulated in the earlier chapter. Hence, in this aim in professional education, the level of the learning that should occur or is expected of the recruits to the profession is considered. Hegarty (1976: 81) points out that legal education

> can easily degenerate into mindless book learning. . . any student of university calibre could obtain a comfortable honours degree by doing little more than memorising the set text-book in each subject and doing the very occasional problem.

Clearly this is not an ideal situation and completion of a course of this nature is not satisfying the aim of professional education. District nursing has recently sought to overcome a similar problem by setting the final written examination paper with three parts: each pitched at a different level on Bloom's taxonomy of educational objectives in the cognitive domain. Bloom (1956) suggested that the lower order objectives are: knowledge, comprehension and application while the higher order objectives are synthesis, analysis and evaluation of know-ledge. The ability to use the knowledge taught and learned in professional education is fundamental, so that a critical aware-ness of the content is an important element in the professional curriculum.

Therefore, it may be seen from the above, that the aims of professional education form a basis for discussion about some criteria for selecting the content of the curriculum. However, the student is being prepared to enter professional practice, so that the demands of this constitute a second set of criteria for the selection of curriculum content.

The Demands of Professional Practice

The role of the professional practitioner is often a very complex one and isolating the various demands of practice is extremely difficult. It may be necessary to undertake an empirical study of the practice of a random sample of practitioners in order to get a thorough understanding of the various factors involved in it. Yet even a study such as this might not reveal the total role of the practitioner or may be biased in some manner, so that however sophisticated the research project it may not form a perfect basis upon which to construct a curriculum. Even if it were, it would reveal only how the role is played rather than how leading professionals consider it ought to be played. Additionally, research provides no criteria for selecting which interpretation of the role researched is more near that of the 'perfect' practitioner. Since there is no intrinsic logical connec-tion between what is and what ought to be, such empirical research can provide guidelines only upon which the curriculum content may be selected. Such research would be a useful undertaking when considering what the new recruit to a profession might be expected to learn during the course of his initial education.

It might be claimed that the objections already stated invalidate the necessity for undertaking such an empirical investigation. But, in response to this, it might be asked whether there is any other way to ensure that a new entrant to a profession learns or is taught, knowledge, skills and attitudes relevant to his future practice other than through an actual study of the practice. Many teachers in the professions, or even administrators of the professions, who were once practitioners, might claim that as a result of their own experience in practice, their current experience adjacent to practice and their own professional knowledge they know what the work entails and, therefore, what should be included in the curriculum. Yet the practice of an occupation is not static; knowledge, skills and attitudes change; perceptions alter when individuals change position; their own experience may not be typical: thus it may be seen that the ex-practitioners may be in no position to specify or highlight the current demands of practice. Yet it may be impossible to undertake a sophisticated sociological survey in order to isolate all the tasks of the practitioner so that all the demands of professional practice might be reflected in the content incorporated in the curriculum. But the professional practitioners are clearly in a better position than either the teachers or the administrators of a profession to spotlight these demands and should, therefore, be involved in the construction of professional education curricula.

'Demands' remains a very wide concept and yet, at the outset, this appears a more relevant concept than that of professional needs. However, later in this section there will be some discussion of 'needs' although it does not form a central feature in understanding criteria for the selection of content, as its prevalence in educational theory would perhaps suggest that it ought. 'Demands' has been used here to relate specifically to the fulfilment of the second aim of professional education formulated in the previous chapter: in order to achieve that aim, certain expectations must be met and in this instance they stem from the requirements of professional practice. However, in order for any new recruits to a profession to be able to enter professional practice successfully, the content of their basic professional education should equip them to respond to these demands. Therefore, other criteria for selection of curriculum content become apparent and each of these must be recognised in relation to these demands. Included in these criteria are: validity, relevance, worthwhileness, needs, balance, breadth and depth. Each of these will now be analysed briefly:

Validity. For knowledge, skills and attitudes to be valid, they must be considered by the curriculum designers and the assessors of that curriculum to be sound and defensible. This does not mean that they must be 'true' because the assertion of 'truth' implies that there is a correct answer to a problem, interpretation of a phenomenon, etc. and this is manifestly not so. Nevertheless, there may be times when there is a correct, or true piece of knowledge, e.g. an interpretation given by a specific legal ruling to the meaning of a law, the dosage of a drug to be administered according to a specific authority. Therefore, this form of truth may also be included within this broader concept of 'validity'. Knowledge, skills and attitudes might be valid but not relevant, so that validity in itself does not constitute sufficient reason for inclusion of these topics in the curriculum of professional education.

Relevance. Like validity, relevance is a relative rather than absolute criterion. Since professional practice is constantly undergoing change as a result of new knowledge being introduced and new techniques being adopted, curricula must change in relation to innovation in practice. If they fail to do so, they quickly become outmoded and irrelevant. As a writer in the Times Higher Educational Supplement (21 Jan. 1978: 16) described this change:

> rhetoric, a vital intellectual skill in the classical world, is a dead discipline today while theology, the central academic tradition in medieval universities, has only a precarious existence on the fringes of higher education in our present society.

Rhetoric may be relevant to both barristers and clergy and theology to the latter, yet neither occupy an important place in the majority of curricula, even though they did so once. The relevance of a discipline to the practice of the profession is an important factor in deciding what should be included within a professional education curriculum.

Relevance implies that some knowledge, skills and attitudes are given more value than others. Clearly this must be the case within the context of selecting content. Yet the value placed upon it is only derived and relative rather than unique and absolute. Nevertheless, there is a sense in which relevant knowledge is seen as valuable because it is relevant, even though knowledge in itself may have no value.

Worthwhileness. Peters construes one of the central characteristics of education to be the transmission of that which is considered worthwhile. This claim was not accepted earlier and it was suggested that 'worthwhileness' is a criterion for the selection of curriculum content rather than a necessary criterion for education per se. It is unnecessary to rehearse this discussion to any greater length than has already been undertaken.

It is, however, hard to deny that 'worthwhileness' is a
criterion for selection of content since both the development of
a person and of a professional person should occur through the
process of education. It is illogical to claim that a subject or
topic has been included in the curriculum because it is not
worthwhile learning it. Hence, it is easy to understand why it
is often claimed that the process of education is valuable since
those who undertake it successfully usually regard it as having
been a worthwhile enterprise. By contrast, unsuccessful negotiation of the process may evoke less supportive reactions, so
that evaluation of the process may best be considered as a subjective assessment undertaken by individuals from their differing
perspectives.

Even so, specific topics might be included in the curriculum
because those planning it consider the study of these subjects
to be a worthwhile enterprise; Pellegrino (1977), for instance,
in proposing that medical students should also study the
humanities was implying that he considered this to be a worthwhile enterprise. Foundation years in a number of courses often
offer students the opportunity to study more widely than merely
in their specialist, or vocational, disciplines because it is widely
accepted as being valuable for people to have studied forms of
knowledge other than those directly relevant to their academic
or professional practice.

It has been claimed in this study that education is essentially
a humanistic enterprise, so that it seems logical to suppose that
any subject selected for inclusion in the curriculum should lead
to the development of the participants as well as to their
professional development. As mentioned above, it would be
illogical to claim that a subject has been included in the curriculum, even though the study of it would not be worthwhile to the
participants. Hence it may be asked why worthwhileness is not
considered to be a characteristic of education per se and the
response must be that a distinction should be made between
the learning process itself and the value placed upon the content
to be learned; worthwhile, in this context, refers to the latter
only.

Needs. This term has also been fairly fully discussed earlier and
it would be tedious to repeat much of what has gone before.
Nevertheless, it was suggested that 'needs' are not a basis for
the aims of education in general so much as a criterion for incor-
poration of different topics in the curriculum. The definition of
the concept of need is shrouded in educational literature,
although Lawson (1975: 37) has suggested that whenever 'a
deficiency can be remedied by the help of some educational
process' an educational need has been established. It is, therefore, possible to regard 'needs' as a criterion for the selection
of the curriculum in professional education, especially in professional continuing education. It is important to this discussion
to recognise that the concept of 'need' by itself is hardly utilis-

able, so that it is necessary to extend the analysis. One way by
which this can be undertaken is by recognising that needs
become apparent in different ways. Bradshaw (1977) demonstrated
this by suggesting that four types appear: normative, felt,
expressed and comparative. Normative needs refer to the recognition of imbalance, hence deficiency, has occurred that can be
rectified before a person, or persons, achieves a desirable
standard. The needs may be defined by the 'expert' who may be
the educator of professionals or an employer as manager of
professionals. In these instances it is legitimate to plan a course,
or part of a course, based upon these needs recognised and
expressed by the 'expert' when examining the professional performance of a number of practitioners. However, many professional performances may not be open to such examination,
laggards may escape attention for many years in professional
practice.

Felt needs exist amongst professionals when they are aware
that they are deficient in knowledge or skill because, for some
reason or other, they have been unable to learn about some
aspect of their professional practice. In some instances the practitioner may not express this need because, perhaps, he might
have felt that acknowledging a deficiency openly is 'unprofessional'. Nevertheless, when professionals are aware that they
have a deficiency, continuing education modules may be constructed in order to rectify it. Recognition that curricula are
built in part, upon the felt or expressed needs of professionals
indicates that it is not always the educator's prerogative to
prepare the course programme, based upon his own professional
awareness. It also suggests that educators in the professions
should be in close contact with professionals in the field so that
appropriate responses may be made to felt and expressed need.

Bradshaw's final type of need is comparative need: unless
professionals practise in teams, i.e. group practice in medicine
or the multidisciplinary primary health care team, the awareness
of need by comparison is much less likely to occur. Nevertheless,
if it does then a similar process might occur as in the case of
felt and expressed need, so that no further discussion is
necessary at this point.

The needs of the professional's own client have been cited
already and it may be that, in continuing education, these would
constitute a valid basis for including material in the curriculum.
For instance, a course on maternal care in midwifery continuing
education might benefit immensely from discussing with new
mothers what were their felt needs so that these might be incorporated in the curriculum.

It is, therefore, claimed here that needs may be a criterion
for the selection of topics for a curriculum or syllabus in professional education, especially in continuing education. It may
be noticed that the needs of the educators themselves have not
been mentioned but it is claimed here that the educator's own
needs do not constitute a basis for incorporating topics into the

curriculum. Yet this may be seen to conflict with the idea of academic freedom, since it might be claimed that the academic is free to include within the curriculum that he teaches what he thinks should be included, or what he wants to include. But while the academie, being the master of his theoretical discipline, may be free to include within it that which he considers should be learned he should do so responsibly, and in professional education, the demands of the practice and the satisfaction of the needs of the client are more important than the needs of the teacher. Additionally, the academic is not intrinsic to the process of education whereas the learner is, so that the learner's needs constitute a valid basis for the selection of topics for the curriculum, whereas the teacher's do not.

The concept of needs remains a complex one and no attempt has been made here to explore it in more than an introductory manner. However, it is clear that once it is recognised that needs may form one criterion in the selection of curriculum content it has other ramifications, such as who designs the course programme and the professionalism of educator and of the learners. Some of these issues are referred to elsewhere in this study.

Balance. The balance of the curriculum always requires some consideration. Already reference has been made to the balance between theory and practice: whether the course will produce students whose academic training has been all-embracing but whose practical experience is minimal, whether the reverse has occurred, or whether the recruit has expertise in both. Hence, the relationship between theory and practice requires careful consideration.

There is, also, another element of balance and that is the extent to which the different elements of professional education, included in Table 3.1, are divided in such a manner as to result in the fulfilment of the aims of professional education.

The balance of a course is something that experienced professional educators will tend to be aware of and to a considerable extent, when they have freedom of design of the course, it remains their responsibility. Nevertheless, this responsibility requires that they should constantly monitor the course that they organise and teach, so that they can be responsive to the demands of professional practice.

Breadth of Knowledge, Skills and Attitudes. Closely related to the idea of balance is that of breadth. Curricula that are narrow tend to incorporate only those aspects of a professional practitioner's work that occur frequently. However, there are the rarer occurrences which require his consideration and while, obviously, it is impossible to teach students about every eventuality that they will encounter in practice, courses in professional education need to be broad enough to equip the students to be able to respond to the less common demands of practice.

Depth of Knowledge. The final criterion for selection of curriculum content to be discussed here is 'depth' or 'level' of knowledge. An aim of professional education, it was suggested earlier, is for learners to develop a critical awareness of the subject taught, so that this means the knowledge, skills and attitudes included in the curriculum are not beyond dispute. Hence the subject must be taken to, at least, sufficient depth to allow the learners to develop a critical approach to what they learn. Failure to encourage students to do this lessens the ideals of professional education and even of education itself.

This first part of the chapter has sought to examine criteria for selection of curriculum content and it has drawn together the aims of education, the demands of professional practice and a number of other criteria that require discussion. However, it was pointed out earlier in this chapter that once an examination syllabus has been prepared, a curriculum published by the professional bodies or an agreement reached with a validating body other criteria obtain in the actual teaching situation. In addition, some of the points already raised take on additional significance, so that the second part of this chapter examines criteria for selection of curriculum content in the actual educational process.

REASONS FOR INCORPORATING SPECIFIC CONTENT IN THE CURRICULUM

Professional schools, departments in universities and polytechnics are rarely totally free from the demands of the professional body as well as from the demands of professional practice. In some instances, professions stipulate quite categorically the minimum examination syllabus and regularly inspect the schools to ensure that the school is teaching the appropriate material, to an acceptable standard. In others, usually university and polytechnic departments, the professional body and the educational institution agree upon what is to be taught, as a result of a submission from the latter to the former. In both of these instances different criteria apply for teaching the subjects taught and this constitutes the first sub-section of this part of the chapter. Finally, other criteria that obtain in the teaching and learning situation are examined.

Duty, Contract and Responsibility

In relation to the actual teaching and learning situation, there often exists either a published examination syllabus, e.g. the General Nursing Council makes such recommendations for the state registration examination of nurses, or a curriculum that has been agreed between the professional body and the educational institution. In the case of the former, especially when the teachers are themselves employed in the examining profession, as they are in schools of nursing and the Law Society's schools, they have a duty to cover the content stipulated in the examination syllabus. That duty may not entail that precisely everything is covered in equal depth or that an equal amount of time should be spent on every subject, but it does mean that the teacher has been employed to teach a specific course. It might be claimed that the existence of an examination syllabus is no reason why the teacher should actually follow it if he considers it more beneficial for his students to learn other topics. Clearly there is no logical reason why the teacher should have this duty, especially if he considers that the stipulated content of the examination syllabus does not allow him to achieve the educational aims suggested earlier. Nevertheless, unless the students are able to satisfy the profession by satisfactorily negotiating the examinations set by it, they will never be able to enter the profession. Since the teacher also has a responsibility to his students it may reinforce the duty he has to teach the topics stipulated in the syllabus. However, this does not mean that teachers having both this duty and responsibility should merely include in the educational process that content stipulated by the professions. They may teach the students to become as critically aware of the syllabus as they themselves may be, without producing students who merely reflect their views. Additionally, they may incorporate into their own syllabii other aspects of knowledge, skills and attitudes that, from their own professional awareness and research, they think ought to be learned.

Merely to teach critical awareness of, and add to, the topics taught is not sufficient to fulfil the teacher's duty to the profession in those cases where he disagrees with the stipulated examination syllabus. It is incumbent upon him to share his views with his colleagues in the profession, to have them examined by his peers and also to endeavour to have the examination syllabus amended accordingly. However, this is to deviate from the crux of this discussion - that the teacher has a duty to the profession and a responsibility to his students to ensure that any examination syllabus is covered during the educational process, so that his students have at least an equal chance as students from other similar professional educational institutions of successfully negotiating whatever examination system prevails.

By contrast, in many instances a contract exists between the profession and the educational institutions which is sealed as a result of the professional body approving a course submission made by the educational institution. This approval may be for a specified period, such as five years, during which time the educational institution teaches and examines the candidates. Sometimes the professional qualification is awarded along with the university's own award of degree or diploma, etc. or in other cases separate examinations may be set. In law, for instance, students with a law degree have been exempted from part or whole of Part I of both the Law Society and the Bar examinations but in other professions there has been an even greater amount of co-operation so that students who pass a university qualification are then entitled to register as a qualified member of the profession. However, the point of this discussion is to highlight the fact that the professional body has approved the submission which will include certain specified curriculum content. Having entered a contract to teach that material, academics at these institutions should abide by their contract, as a matter of duty. Naturally, contracts can be changed, they frequently are if the approval is for a limited period only, but once the contract has been entered it should be kept. In this instance, since the academics also examine the students there is no other reason for keeping the contract than that of having made it.

Clearly the relationship between the professions and the institutions of higher education in the United Kingdom is complex. Hegarty (1976: 84) for instance, says that this is an abiding problem in law education:

> I feel, therefore, that the relationship of the universities and the polytechnics to the professional requirements of law practice has not yet been fully worked out. Some considerable advances towards a more rational relationship are in process of being made at present . . .

When this relationship is made clear, it may be that the ethics of the contract between the profession and the university will be more clearly worked out for legal education. Nevertheless, it is more clear for other professions and having reached an agreement upon the content of the curriculum, it is the moral duty of those who teach to ensure that those topics are covered and as a result mutual trust should emerge between the professions and institutions of higher education.

Yet the content of the curriculum, agreed or stipulated by the profession, is not the only criterion for inclusion in the actual teaching and learning process, so that the final section of this chapter examines other criteria.

Other Criteria for the Selection of Curriculum Content in the Educational Process

Thus far, criteria for selection of curriculum content in relation to the preparation of the curriculum and in relation to agreed or stipulated curriculum have been examined, but the final area of consideration is that which relates to the learners themselves in the actual educational process. Three separate criteria are discussed here: previous experience, interests and learnability of the material.

Student's Previous Experience. Malcolm Knowles (1978: 56) suggests that one of the major assumptions of andragogy (the

theory and practice of teaching adults) is consideration of the
role of the adult student's own experience. Knowles is more
concerned with the actual techniques of teaching and in this
instance andragogy will be discussed in Chapter 6, but the
concern here is with the philosophical criteria of including content in the curriculum. Nevertheless, Knowles (1978: 56) raises
a significant point as to why this is an important criterion in
adult teaching:

> (The adult) increasingly defines who he is by his experience.
> To a child, experience is something that happens to him; to
> an adult, his experience is WHO HE IS. So in any situation in
> which an adult's experience is being devalued or ignored, the
> adult perceives this as not rejecting just his experience but
> rejecting him as a person. Andragogues convey their respect
> for people by making use of their experience as a resource for
> learning.

While Knowles (1980) has retracted his exclusive claims for
andragogy, he still raises some significant issues. Even in the
above quotation it is possible to dispute his clear demarcation
between the child and the adult and yet the thrust of his argument is important. There must be opportunity in courses for
adults, like those in professional education, for adults to utilise
their experience and to build upon it. The curriculum should
give opportunity to adult learners for this to occur and the
process itself should be of an adult nature, as was suggested in
the discussion on adult education in the opening chapter, so
that the learner's own personal development may continue.
Additionally, the adult learner's experience in terms of curriculum content should also be recognised, so that repetition of
learning experiences are not expected by students since these
may easily degenerate into an alienating experience from which
the learner withdraws.

Interest. Two aspects of interest require brief discussion here.
First, if the teacher finds a subject interesting he may motivate
students to enjoy it far more than topics which disinterest him.
However professional the teacher may be, his own interests
and concerns need not be hidden from the students, although
the teacher's interest does not constitute sufficient reason for
its taking precedence over other topics in the curriculum. The
student's interest, however, may constitute a reason for spend-
ing additional time on a topic during the course. Nevertheless,
if a student's interest is likely to unbalance his study programme,
then the teacher might have to prevent this occurring. At the
same time, it should be recognised that in self-directed learning
the student may plough his own furrows through the fields of
knowledge which start from his own interests and develop
thereafter. Hence the learner's interest should at least constitute
one criterion in considering the content of the curriculum.

Learnability. Coupled closely with interest is the learnability of the topic. It has been demonstrated that individuals learn better if they can make links between what they already know and what they are about to learn. Students should be able to connect new knowledge to existing knowledge and this, to some extent, should act as a guiding principle in deciding upon the progression of curriculum content.

CONCLUSION

This chapter has attempted to examine briefly some of the reasons why specific content should be included in the curriculum. It started by linking the reasons to the aims of professional education and has related this to the demands of professional practice. It then recognised that the alliance between professions and educational institutions created another set of criteria that required examination within the context of any specific educational process. Finally, it has suggested that within the teaching and learning situation certain criteria pertaining to the students also need consideration. No single criterion may be claimed to dominate and most are relevant to every situation.

Thus far curriculum content and knowledge, skills and attitudes have been used almost synonymously, but it is now necessary to examine the concepts in greater detail, especially the relationship of knowledge to skills and attitudes in professional education.

Earlier it was claimed that underlying every profession is a
body of knowledge and that, in some ways, the occupation
endeavoured to control the application of that knowledge in
practice. The practice of the occupation, however, demands
more than the mere possession of theoretical knowledge since
this alone does not result in competency. Hence, it is now
necessary to examine in some depth the elements of professional
competency that were mentioned in the third chapter. Initially,
the concepts of knowledge, skill and attitude are examined
separately but it is necessary to understand their interrelationship. Additionally, in this chapter, these concepts are related
to professionalisation, professionalism and continuing education.

KNOWLEDGE AND THE PROFESSIONS

The concept of knowledge has occupied the minds of philosophers
throughout the history of the discipline and no attempt is made
here to chronicle this debate nor even to refer to all the eminent
writers on the topic. It is intended here, however, to examine
briefly the meaning of the word and thereafter to discuss: ways
of arriving at knowledge; levels, types and forms of knowledge;
research and the development of knowledge; knowledge as a
changing phenomenon and professionalisation, professionalism
and continuing education, the concept of professional knowledge;
professional knowledge and education.

The Concept of Knowledge

An English dictionary reveals how a word is used in common
speech and provides clues as to its conceptual meaning. Collins
'Dictionary of the English Language' defines knowledge thus:

> 1. the facts, feelings and experiences known by a person or
> a group of people. 2. the state of knowing. 3. awareness,
> consciousness or familiarity gained by experience or learning.
> 4. evaluation or informed learning. 5. specific information
> about a subject. 6. sexual intercourse (. . . carnal know-
> ledge). 7. to come to one's knowledge . . . 8. to my . . .
> knowledge . . . (1979: 813)

A number of these definitions are tautologous and therefore

throw no new light on the meaning of the word, but those numbered 3-5 offer a useful starting point and also raise a major issue. The third and fourth definitions imply that knowledge is subjective, gained through the senses as a result of individual and social experiences, whereas the fifth offers the possibility of there being objective knowledge. It may be asked, therefore, whether information about a specific subject stored on a computer file or in a book is actually knowledge, or therefore, whether knowledge can exist without the human mind to 'know' it. A response might be that the information written in a book is the codification of a writer's knowledge and data that might become knowledge for a reader, but in its book form it is merely recorded data. The same argument does not hold good if the computer has been programmed to generate new information from different sets of data. If the information on a specific subject is totally new then it has never existed in a human mind and, consequently, it has never been knowledge. 'Specific information about a subject' may not, therefore, always be knowledge, only potential knowledge. Without entering into the debate about 'objective knowledge' (Popper 1972) it is suggested here that until information has been processed by the human mind it is not knowledge, and knowledge only becomes knowledge for an individual when he or she has processed it. However, this argument tends to suggest that the mere fact of processing data in the human mind generates knowledge; it implies that the mind is no more than the receptacle of the information. But this is not so. Earlier it was argued that there has to be active participation in the learning process and an understanding of what is internalised. It is now possible to suggest that the mind may synthesise diverse sets of sense experiences and create new knowledge which is understood by the possessor. Knowledge, then, is the product of the mind.

Berger and Luckmann (1967: 13) suggest that knowledge is 'the certainty that phenomena are real and that they possess certain characteristics'. While they recognise that the philosopher will immediately enquire as to how the certainty was reached and whether there is reality, they maintain that such a definition might be acceptable both to the philosopher and to the man in the street. Clearly the word 'real' poses several problems, since a theoretical perspective or a rationalistic argument may appear to be removed from reality, in as much as 'reality' appears to imply something actual, almost tangible and objectified rather than conceptual. Hence, the problems presented by this terminology suggest that the definition needs amendment if it is to fulfil the hopes that Berger and Luckmann had for it. By contrast, Hirst (1974: 85) suggests that the domain of knowledge is not the certainty of phenomena but 'true propositions or statements' which overcomes some of the objections to Berger and Luckmann's definition, but raises other problems about truth and certainty. Must knowledge always be true? Is truth absolute or relative? If the knower is certain but found to be wrong, did he actually possess knowledge?

In the light of new discoveries and rapidly changing perspectives it might be argued that some types of knowledge, e.g. technological knowledge, are only true in relation to the present state of the discipline. The knowledge statement which is considered true in one era might be regarded as obsolete in another, and even false. But can knowledge be false? The mere fact that false knowledge or incorrect knowledge are comprehensible terms implies that all knowledge possessed by an individual has not necessarily to be true, nor need it be true all the time. An individual's knowledge might have rested upon incorrect or incomplete data, incorrect interpretation of data, etc. so that it could have resulted in incorrect knowledge. Hence, if the individual is circumspect in the way that he interprets information and tentative in the way he presents his knowledge, he may actually be able to present more correct knowledge, albeit knowledge qualified by the constraints of the manner in which data was collected and interpreted. It was considerations such as these that led Ayer (1956: 35) to conclude that:

> the necessary and sufficient conditions for knowing that something is the case are first that what one is said to know be true, secondly that one be sure of it, and thirdly that one should have the right to be sure.

Thus knowledge may best be defined in terms of the relationship between the awareness of the phenomenon and the experience that leads to it. A working definition adopted here is a modification of the third definition taken from the dictionary and quoted earlier. Knowledge may be seen as a level of awareness, consciousness or familiarity gained by experience, learning or thinking. Before discussing this in any more detail it is necessary now to examine the ways of achieving this state of consciousness.

Methods of Arriving at Knowledge

Scheffler (1965) highlights the three broad philosophical approaches to knowledge: rationalist, empiricist and pragmatic. Each of these are important, not only because of the additional perspectives that they present to knowledge but because they also indicate how it may be taught and learned in the educational process. Knowledge arrived at through the principles of rationalism is not greatly dependent upon the environment but rests upon the process of pure reason. The mathematician for instance, requires no empirical evidence nor does he need quantitative data. Through the logical processes of reason he may probe from his initial premise until he reaches a conclusion. Provided the original premise was demonstrably true and the logical process correct then the conclusion must be true knowledge.

Natural and social phenomena are explored by experience. The educator, for instance, may be sure that members of his class have specific learning needs because he has observed their anxiety during a lesson. An astronomer may understand something more of the solar system because he has observed empirical data. Knowledge based upon empirical evidence may reflect an understanding of a past pheomenon but may never logically be employed to predict a future one.

Pragmatism, however, implies that knowledge is gained as a result of experimentation. The individual may reach a certain level of belief as a result of his observations of a phenomenon, but the hypothesis has to be tested and tried. Experimentation, trial and error, are the experiences through which the validity of knowledge is examined.

Each of these approaches to knowledge is different; each depends upon a correct use of the method of acquiring the data and processing it into knowledge. If the method is inadequate or the process incorrect then the resulting conclusions may be false knowledge. Hence the context in which knowledge is acquired is relevant to its expression. Additionally, it may be that no method actually exists to ascertain the validity of a statement. Then it may be considered to be a belief rather than actual knowledge, an idea resting upon circumstantial or inconclusive evidence rather than upon logic, fact or demonstrable experimentation.

These different approaches suggest that knowledge itself is not a homogeneous unity but rather that there may be different forms.

Types, Forms and Levels of Knowledge

Knowledge, as it has been presented here, appears to be subjective rather than objective: that is, that knowledge is only knowledge when it has been internalised by the human mind. Before that time, only the actual constituent elements of knowledge exist and these have continuity without the human mind. For instance, the physical phenomena that are the raw materials for empirical and some pragmatic knowledge exist independently of the mind. Cultural knowledge, folk knowledge, etc. built up through the generations and passed from one generation to the next appears to be objective, merely because of its commonality and unchangeableness. The raw material of knowledge is stored in books and computers and was probably once some person's knowledge. When it is learned by another it will become their knowledge. But before it is actually learned it is only potential knowledge. That it appears to have a life of its own by virtue of the process of being transmitted gives it the appearance of objectivity. Yet it is only an appearance. It is objectified rather than objective. Nevertheless, objectified knowledge may be treated as if it is objective in some ways and the very use of language lends knowledge some semblance of objectivity.

Thus it is possible to treat knowledge as if it were an objective reality and the body of knowledge may be regarded as the sum total of human knowledge shared or stored by humanity. Professional knowledge may, therefore, be seen as that selection from the body of knowledge that is regarded by specific members of an occupation as being the base upon which that occupation's practice is founded. It may be that some of that body of knowledge overlaps with that claimed by another occupation, since it is impossible to envisage discrete bodies of professional knowledge. But it was pointed out earlier that professional practitioners require both knowledge and skill and it is possible to subdivide knowledge into two types, traditionally - 'knowledge that' and 'knowledge how'. The former relates to propositions of accepted validity, while the latter suggests an awareness or familiarity with process or technique. These two types of knowledge may form a part of the basis of the education and training of professionals. Since the next main section of this chapter concentrates upon skills and incorporates a discussion about 'knowledge how', 'knowledge that' will be considered at this juncture.

Since 'knowledge that' is objectified, it may be discussed as if it were objective and, consequently, divided into forms and disciplines. Hirst's (1974: 25) seven forms of knowledge (mathematics, physical sciences, knowledge of persons, literature and the fine arts, morals, religion and philosophy) are, he claims, fundamentally distinct and irreducible categories of knowledge as evidenced by the concepts, logical propositions employed and criteria for truth in the terms by which they are assessed. He has rejected a fourth criterion, which is the methodology employed for amassing truth prepositions (1974: 85ff). In various papers he has sought to demonstrate that this classification is one that may be employed with different disciplines although he specifically rejects that this is a discipline-based classification. It is significant to note here that 'knowledge that', knowledge of persons, moral and philosophical knowledge all occurred in the discussion about professional competence in the third chapter. The result of broadening the curriculum in this manner, Hirst argues, is that the basis for the development of a logical mind is created. However, it is beyond the scope of this chapter to analyse Hirst's formulation in a more critical manner.

This formulation, whilst not specifically based on the disciplines, does at least point to the differentiation of knowledge and clearly knowledge may be divided into the disciplines as well as into forms. The academic disciplines are based upon the manner by which the knowledge is gained as well as upon the interrelationship between truth, theory and problem. Unlike Hirst's forms of knowledge, the academic disciplines are not discrete and they appear to be more like a spectrum in which each colour fuses into the next. However, the use of the disciplines allows the learner to focus upon the phenomenon under investigation from a specific perspective and thus to understand it in depth. A similar argument might be mounted for a thematic approach towards phenomena and it may be argued that this is how the majority of people seek to comprehend an object or a process. While this claim may be true, it is not the way that has generally been employed in academic study, so that the discipline-based approach may be more likely to prevail in professional education since, as many occupations are professionalising, they seek to locate their education and training in the sphere of higher education.

In the process of learning knowledge, it is also important to recognise that there are different levels of learning. One of the aims of professional education, it was claimed in the third chapter, is that the learner should understand the knowledge that is learned. Clearly it would appear illogical for a student to claim to know something but not to understand it. Yet it sometimes occurs that rote learning does not lead to comprehension. Hence it was claimed earlier that to understand knowledge implied that the learner is able to differentiate between true and false knowledge and to reject the latter. Understanding is used here in a much broader manner than that employed by Bloom and his associates (1956) in devising their well known taxonomy of educational objectives in the cognitive domain. They suggested that there are six levels of knowledge:

(1) To have knowledge – recall of specifics, universals, processes, methods, patterns, structures, etc.
(2) Comprehension – the lowest level of understanding, so that the learner can make use of the knowledge learned.
(3) Application – to be able to use abstractions in both a concrete and particular situation.
(4) Analysis – the breakdown of knowledge into its constituent parts in order to clarify ideas.
(5) Synthesis – the putting together of parts into a whole to reveal new ideas.
(6) Evaluation – judging the value of the knowledge.

Bloom's taxonomy was devised in order to theorise about examinations and has since proved useful.

It might be argued that these levels need not occur in a hierarchical sequence but then Bloom and his associates did view this classification as a taxonomy rather than a hierarchy. Yet this approach does highlight an important factor in teaching and learning, that having knowledge may not be as significant as understanding or assessing it.

Bloom's perspective is not the only one employed by learning theorists about levels of learning, although it is probably the most explicit one in relation to knowledge itself. Gagné (1977) produced a hierarchical model of learning in which there are eight levels: signal learning, stimulus-response learning, motor and verbal chaining, multiple discrimination, concept learning, rule learning and problem solving. It is important to note that this approach is an analysis of the learning process rather than the level at which the knowledge is learned and it is, thus, a slightly different approach.

Knowledge, then, is not a simple nor homogeneous phenomenon: it is complex and problematic. Yet knowledge is not a static phenomenon. In an age which has witnessed a knowledge explosion, it is dynamic and needs now to be considered from this perspective.

Research and the Development of Knowledge

Many occupations that view themselves as professions take one of the criteria of their professionalisation to be institutionalised research: they claim to be research-based occupations. The extent to which the claim is valid may be less significant to this discussion than it might be to the sociologist seeking empirical evidence to support or refute it. The more an occupation encourages any form of research of an empirical or pragmatic nature and the more thinkers are enjoined to consider rationally the state of the knowledge base of an occupation, consequently the more that knowledge base will grow. Yet it is implicit in discussion that knowledge resulting from empirical or pragmatic investigation may change more rapidly than that having a rationalistic foundation. Hence the 'knowledge that' form of knowledge may change much more rapidly than those other forms, i.e. knowledge of persons, morals and philosophy, claimed to be significant to professional practice.

Scheler (cited in Merton 1968: 524ff) claimed that different forms of knowledge changed at varying rates, so that knowledge embedded in the culture of society is likely to change less rapidly than some other forms. He classified knowledge which undergoes rapid transformation as being artifical.

On a continuum from slow to rapid rates of change, he isolated seven different forms of knowledge:

(1)   Myth and legend.
(2)   Knowledge implicit in national folk language.
(3)   Religious knowledge.
(4)   Basic forms of mystical knowledge.
(5)   Philosophical metaphysical knowledge.
(6)   Positive knowledge of mathematics, natural and cultural knowledge.
(7)   Technological knowledge.

Whether his classes of knowledge are quite as discrete as those formulated by Hirst is debatable, yet the rationale underlying his argument is undeniable. Clearly technological knowledge and positive knowledge change faster than folk knowledge. Hence the knowledge bases of many professional occupations are likely to undergo rapid change.

The process of rapidly changing knowledge is bound to have two major effects: initially, it may cause new sub-disciplines to appear in the spectrum of knowledge and, secondly, it may produce new forms of professional occupation based upon the new sub-disciplines or upon new combinations of sub-disciplines. Berger and Luckmann (1967: 95) summarise this:

> Given the historical accumulation of knowledge in a society, we can assume that, because of the division of labour, role specific knowledge will grow at a faster rate than generally relevant and accessible knowledge. The multiplications of specific tasks brought about by the division of labour requires standardized solutions that can be readily learned and transmitted. These in turn require specialized knowledge of certain situations, and of the means/ends relationships in terms of which the situations are socially defined. In other words, specialists will arise, each of whom will have to know whatever is deemed necessary for the fulfilment of his particular task.

Thus the more research is instituted in any society or occupation, the greater the body of knowledge that will be produced and stored and that professionals will be expected to learn. Hence, the period of initial professional education may lengthen as it is deemed necessary for the new recruit to learn more and more knowledge before he is allowed to enter practice. Continuing education will also become institutionalised and yet it will still be difficult to keep abreast with all the new knowledge being generated in any specific field. This produces more specialists and more specialisms, so that eventually new occupations and professions emerge and new professional curricula are formulated.

Knowledge as a Changing Phenomenon and Professionalisation, Professionalism and Continuing Education

Professional knowledge cannot, therefore, be regarded as a static phenomenon which means that curricula will have to be adjusted to be relevant to the new developments within the profession. An implication of this for the teacher of professionals is that he should also keep abreast with all new knowledge that appears within his profession. The teacher's own professionalism is discussed later, so that it is not elaborated upon here. Suffice to note though the need of the teacher to specialise since it may be impossible to keep abreast with the body of knowledge underlying the whole of a profession.

Hence it is logical to anticipate that as the amount of knowledge becomes too complex so it will divide into new sub-disciplines and, similarly, fission occurs in professions: new occupations emerge as new sub-disciplines and specialisms appear. It is therefore unwise to consider the occupation or profession as a static entity and Bucher and Strauss (cited in Vollmer and Mills 1966: 186) actually suggest, as stated earlier, that 'professions are loose amalgamations of segments pursuing different objectives in different manners and more or less delicately held together under a common name at a particular period in history'. As different segments emerge, they seek to demarcate that body of knowledge relevant to their own professional practice and to educate and train their own practitioners in it. With the appearance of the different branches of a profession, the process of professionalisation may recommence for each, in a manner similar to that described by Wilensky and discussed in the second chapter of this text.

There is, therefore, an intrinsic relationship between the rapidity in the rate of change of the knowledge, fission in professions and the recommencement of the process of professionalisation.

In a similar manner to the teacher of professionals, the practitioner may be swamped by the body of knowledge being developed by his own professional occupation. The more that research is mounted and the results published, the greater the amount of knowledge the practitioner may consider necessary to know in order to practise his occupation in a competent manner. The greater his commitment to his profession, the more he will feel that he needs to know. Obviously this will result in specialisation where that is possible, but even then, his professionalism will demand that he undertake programmes of continuing education. Traditionally, professional associations have organised conferences and seminars to cater for this demand but, as the amount of knowledge multiplies, the greater will be the demand for continuing education. This will increasingly become the responsibility of the training schools, institutions of higher education, polytechnics and universities, which should alter the whole approach to the life and work of such establishments and help to change them from institutions for the education of young adults to institutions concerned with lifelong education.

Traditionally, sabbatical leave has been restricted to a few professional occupations, but the greater the amount of knowledge generated and the more rapidly that knowledge changes, the more important it will be for professional practitioners to have secondment from their work in order to study. However, the full-time, in-service course is not the only design for continuing education programmes: other structures, for example weekend-schools, summer schools, distance learning, etc., are also possible.

Hence, it may be hypothesised that there is a direct correlation between the professionalism of the practitioner and the growth in provision of continuing education. It is, therefore, necessary to consider briefly once again the concept of continuing education.

At the outset of this book, continuing education was viewed as any planned series of learning incidents, beyond initial education, having a humanistic basis, directed towards the participant's learning and understanding. With the growth of new knowledge it becomes more important that the practitioners should continue to learn. What, however, is to happen if the practitioner has no desire to continue to learn? Should he still be allowed to practise? Should he be accredited? These are clearly major questions and ones that professional associations will increasingly need to consider in the future.

Brief consideration is given to this later. However, who should provide continuing education? Should it be the professional school, the professional association or the institutions of higher education? Alford (1980) shows how this problem may lead to power conflict, so that if no policy is devised continuing education in any profession may be haphazard and ad hoc. The benefit of this may be questioned. At the same time, if there is a regular and planned provision of continuing education, it might extend the work of the teacher of professionals or lead to the emergence of yet another specialism - the continuing education professional.

Additionally, it must be recognised that the provision of continuing education is an expensive undertaking. It may be questioned whether any professional occupation can actually afford the expense of ensuring that all of its practitioners are abreast with the latest developments in their field. Indeed, it may be asked whether it is actually necessary for them all to be fully acquainted with the most recent knowledge developed in their own field. This question is a most important one since it might be argued that in any case, this does not now occur and so why should it in the future? Additionally, if the recruits to the profession develop a professional orientation to their work they will purchase books and journals and attend conferences of their own accord in order to keep abreast and, if they do this, there will be less necessity to provide as much institutionalised continuing education as the growth in new research-based knowledge might indicate to be essential. Clearly there is a certain logic in this argument since the need for provision for continuing education may reflect a failure on the part of initial education to produce recruits who have an appropriate professional ideology. By contrast, it could be argued that practitioners, having the desire to keep abreast with new knowledge but not having the time to do so because of their commitment to their clients, are likely to generate a demand for continuing education in accord with the growth in new research-based knowledge. In this case, it may be seen as an indication of the success of initial professional education.

Formal continuing education, for whatever reason, will most certainly be a branch of education for the foreseeable future and will, therefore, be one of the means by which the ever-changing context of professional knowledge will be acquired in the various occupations and professions which have a knowledge base.

The Concept of Professional Knowledge

Professional knowledge is that selection from the overall body of knowledge considered by members of a profession to be the foundation of their practice. Since some elements of this undergo very rapid change it is impossible to demarcate this selection. Any attempt to do so would tend to suggest that the occupation was static and not undergoing the process of professionalisation. Nevertheless, it is possible to indicate some of the forms of knowledge that combine to form professional knowledge, the basis of which is to be found in the elements of professional competency in the third chapter. Professional knowledge consists of: 'knowledge that' (academic disciplines); 'knowledge how' (psycho-motor elements); knowledge of persons; moral values; professional ideology. Clearly these are similar to some of Hirst's forms of knowledge, although no attempt is made here to equate them.

It is important to note that the first two of these forms of professional knowledge are not specified in terms of academic discipline, since professional knowledge may consist of a mixture of disciplines and the constitution changes as occupations professionalise and as the boundaries of the disciplines become less clear as a result of interdisciplinary research.

Goode (1973: 355ff), an American sociologist who has written a number of papers about the professions, describes professional knowledge as having seven major characteristics:

  (i)   Abstract and organised into a codified body of principles.
 (ii)   Applicable, or thought to be applicable, to the concrete problems of living.
(iii)   Thought by the relevant members of society to be able to solve problems.
 (iv)   That the possession of this knowledge means that problems can be solved.
  (v)   Should be created, organised and transmitted by the profession.
 (vi)   The profession should be arbiter over disputes about the validity of technical solutions.
(vii)   The amount of knowledge and the difficulty of its acquisition should be great enough to give the possessor an aura of mystery not given to ordinary people.

Goode is, very clearly, describing the social context of professional knowledge rather than the knowledge itself. Only the first of his seven points relates to the knowledge itself and even then it only specifies the structure of the knowledge rather than its constitution.

It might be useful at this point to illustrate the concept of professional knowledge, using educational knowledge as an example. In education 'knowledge that' occurs as a result of both empirical and pragmatic undertakings. Research into the educational process has helped to generate a body of knowledge about education that it is now generally considered appropriate for intending teachers to learn. 'Knowledge how' underlies the theories of teaching and learning. Knowledge of persons includes understanding the dynamics of classroom interaction, sensitivity in interpersonal relations in respect of the teacher-learner relationship; ethics includes understanding the moral standards expected of the teacher; and philosophy relates to comprehension of and commitment to the ideals of professionalism that have already been described.

Professional Knowledge and Education

Recruits into a profession are expected to have learned professional knowledge before they enter practice, so that the parameters of the concept provide some guidelines to the content of the professional curriculum. Indeed, it might be claimed that the elements of professional knowledge described here provide the minimum content of the professional curriculum. This, therefore, appears wider than the basis of some current profession curricula which is in implicit agreement with the argument of Pellegrino (1977), mentioned in the previous chapter.

Having thus examined the cognitive dimension of professional education, but without discussion of 'knowledge how', it is now necessary to discuss briefly the other two elements: skills and attitudes.

SKILLS AND THE PROFESSIONS

A professional who has mastery of knowledge without the skills to perform his practice is of no more value than one who has skills but not the knowledge. Yet discussions about professions and professionals tend to emphasise cognition and to depreciate the skills component, which is a reflection of the values that members of British society place upon the cognitive domain. Without accepting this evaluation, this section of the chapter begins by analysing 'knowledge how' and then moves to a discussion about skills and the teaching of skills.

'Knowledge How'

It is possible for the professional who has a theoretical orientation to know how but not to be able. The old maxim 'Don't do as I do, do as I say!' might best describe this situation and also to indicate the difference between knowing how and being able to. The educator of professionals might seek to explain to his students how a procedure is implemented but he may not have the ability to practise it. Another practitioner might be able to demonstrate a technique but not know how or why it is

successful. Yet in everyday speech, knowing how to undertake
a certain procedure usually implies that the individual has the
skills to practise it as well as having the knowledge about the
procedure.

This distinction exercised the mind of Ryle (1949), who was
unhappy with the idea that the competent practitioner of skills
rehearses the theory first and then proceeds. Ryle (1949: 32)
maintained that in doing 'something intelligently, i.e. thinking
about what I am doing, I am doing one thing not two'. For him,
knowing how is the same as intelligent performance, and while
intelligent performance is a feature of 'knowing how' it may not
be its sum total. For instance, an individual who has routinised
his practice may not actually think about what he is doing when
he is doing it. He may do it mindlessly. Yet it would be hard to
deny that he does not know how to carry out his procedure
and, if he were asked, he may be able to teach the knowledge
how most competently.

Hence, it is maintained here that there is a definite distinction
between the cognitive domain of 'knowing how' and the skills
domain of being able to perform a specific operation. 'Knowing
how' might be taught within the theoretical part of a professional
curriculum, if it is taught at all! By contrast, the actual
acquisition of the skill constitutes a practical dimension to the
curriculum and one which is sometimes taught by specialist
teachers, such as practical work teachers in district nursing. It
is recognised, however, that a number of professions have not
developed this element in the education and training of their
recruits to a very high level. Initially, this reflects the dominance attributed to cognitive knowledge in the professions. Yet
it might be asked whether the traditional practice of 'sitting by
Nellie' is the most effective method of learning skills, especially
if 'Nellie' is untrained in the art of teaching them.

Skills

A skill is a special ability, often one that is gained only through
training. The concept of training will not be dealt with here
since it will be discussed in the next chapter; ability, however,
is not absolute - there are levels of proficiency and it may be
impossible to decide precisely when a skill has been achieved.
Scheffler (1965: 95) suggests that there are three levels:
competency, proficiency and mastery. He points out that the
average chess player may have the ability to play chess, but
he may be neither a good player nor a master. In competitive
games, like chess, it is possible to delineate levels of achievement that might be a fair reflection of the ability of the player.
Similarly, it may be possible on a production line to measure the
speed and the accuracy of an operator, thereby providing a
basis for assessment of the level of skill. However, this becomes
more difficult when the procedures become longer and more complicated, especially when it also involves personal interaction.

For instance, it is difficult for a trainer of tutors to decide precisely when a trainee educator has actually achieved competency. Hence it may be argued that, in some instances, competency is a subjective evaluation and, therefore, its level lies in the standards of the assessor.

Yet skill, within a professional context, is very clearly not merely the psycho-motor co-ordination of a machine operative. There is more added to it and this extra is a combination of the theoretical 'knowledge how' to carry out the procedure, the 'knowledge that' upon which the occupation is based and the critical understanding of the practitioner. Hence the practitioner is able to think about the process as he undertakes it, he is able to alter direction or employ different techniques if he considers that the situation demands this change. In the professional context, the human capacity for reflection operates, so that the procedure is an interpenetration of thought and action and knowledge and skill. Consequently, it may be a false division to concentrate upon the theory in the training school and then send the recruit out into practice to learn from a skilled practitioner. Rather the education and training of professional practitioners may be more true to the basis of practice if theory and practice were learned concurrently and interrelatedly.

Teaching Skills

Since the next chapter is concerned with educational processes, this sub-section will be brief. Since training is a process that has been widely researched in manual occupations, e.g. Belbin and Belbin (1972), Smith (1977: 187-202), a body of knowledge has emerged about teaching skills that may be viewed as an element of educational knowledge. It is, therefore, important for teachers of recruits to the professions to ensure that this element of educational knowledge is considered and utilised, if appropriate, for the preparation of new entrants to the professions.

ATTITUDES IN PROFESSIONAL EDUCATION

An attitude, according to Allport (1954: 45), is 'a mental and neural state of readiness, organized through experience, exerting a directive or dynamic influence upon the individual's response to all objects and situations with which it is associated'. In a similar manner, Kretch and Crutchfield (1948: 173) defined an attitude as 'an enduring organization of motivational, emotional, perceptual and cognitive processes with respect to some aspect of the individual's world'. Both of these definitions have a number of similar characteristics including: cognitive and affective orientations towards the phenomenon in question and a behavioural tendency towards it. It may, therefore, be

seen that, if the practice of the occupation is the phenomenon
in question, then there are cognitive and affective orientations
towards it. Hence, it will be recalled that, in the third chapter,
knowledge of professionalism and emotive commitment towards it
were both specified. Knowledge of professionalism may be seen
to be a philosophical form of 'knowledge as belief', whilst
emotive commitment to it as an element which is less frequently
discussed. Nevertheless, it does not appear logical to be preparing individuals to enter a professional occupation unless
those recruits are also being encouraged to be committed to
a belief, an ideology, that should ensure that the recruit
endeavours to provide a high standard of service.

Scheffler (1965: 76) regards belief as 'a disposition to act in
certain ways under certain circumstances'. Naturally the problems of what ways and in what circumstances clearly arise here.
But for the professional certain answers emerge; the professional
is committed to the mastery of the knowledge and skills underlying his practice, so that when the circumstances arise he will
be in a position to provide a service. This is an oversimplifi-
cation, perhaps an idealistic one, of the elements of the professional ideology but by placing it within this framework it is
possible to view the discussion on attitudes within a wider
ideological perspective. Yet it must be recognised that even if
the practitioners have acquired and accepted this ideological
orientation towards professional practice there is no guarantee
that the practitioner will retain a high level of professionalism
throughout his career.

The acquisition of acceptable attitudes in the education and
training of professionals has usually been left to the socialisation
process that, while producing a degree of conformity, is haphazard and often unplanned. Conformity through socialisation
and the acquisition of professional attitudes are two totally
different phenomena. Indeed, the acquisition of professional
attitudes does not imply conformity, but it does demand commitment.

It is perhaps significant to recall that, while Bloom's taxonomy
of educational objectives in the cognitive domain has been widely
discussed and used, those in affective domain are not so widely
employed. Krathwohl et al. (1964) suggested that these objectives may be outlined in a hierarchical order: receiving, res-
ponding, valuing, organisation and characterisation by a value
or a value complex. Such a system of objectives may be useful
in helping educators to plan a programme in the affective
domain in professional education.

However, the outcome of commitment, through such a planned
process, does smack of indoctrination. Yet professionalism
demands a degree of commitment, so does it mean that a part
of the preparation of the new professional must include a process
of indoctrination? This should not occur but if it does, it might
be considered immoral. The process of becoming a professional
does not demand conformity nor is it closed-ended. There is an

open-endedness and a fostering of critical awareness that defies the identification of the process with that of indoctrination. The outcome of such commitment may be totally different for individual practitioners - they may become committed to different branches of the occupation, to different locations of practice, to various branches of the knowledge, to different activities, e.g. practice, teaching, research. Hence it is claimed here that this is an educational, rather than indoctrinational, process but it must be recognised that if wrongly practised it might degenerate into indoctrination.

CONCLUSION

Knowledge, skills and attitudes together form the essentials of professional practice. The practitioner who is weak in one of these dimensions is less than a total professional - each, in its own way, is a vital constituent to practice. Consequently these form the bare essential of the curriculum; the education and training of the professional is incomplete unless the curriculum has provided the recruit with the opportunity to learn and acquire competency in all of these spheres. Assessment of the recruit's competency should, in some way, include appraisal of these elements. But the process by which these are learned remains to be discussed, so that the next chapter explores the educational processes utilised in the professions.

It has been recognised that the education process is predominantly a learning process. The definition, offered at the outset of this work, suggested that education is a particular type of learning process, although it is appreciated that there are others that may not be considered educational. The main purpose of this chapter is to focus upon various learning processes and to distinguish between those which are educational and the remainder. Yet before this is undertaken it is necessary to reconsider the original definition within the context of the education of adults, which constitutes the first main section of this chapter. Thereafter, eleven types of learning process are considered and then some philosophical models of teaching are discussed. The chapter concludes with a brief analysis of the relationship between learning and knowledge.

Two major propositions emerge from this chapter: first that not all teaching or learning processes are educational and, secondly, that some of these processes may to some extent deny the humanity of the learner and may, therefore, be considered immoral. It must be recognised that even in the educational processes incidents occasionally occur that might be classified as immoral and these will be noted during the discussion. Hence, it will be emphasised once again that there is a normative dimension to the educational process but that the grounds for it are to be found in the humanity of the learner, rather than in the subject being studied. The humanity of the learner constituted a major element in the initial definition of education, and it is now necessary to return to this.

ANDRAGOGY AND THE EDUCATION OF ADULTS

Education was defined, in the opening chapter, as 'any planned series of incidents, having a humanistic basis, directed towards the participant(s)' learning and understanding'. In this basic definition no reference was made to the age group of the learners, since education can occur at any stage in the life cycle. It can and does, therefore, occur during adulthood. Adult education is usually considered to be a type of education provided by local education authorities for fee-paying adults in their leisure time. Hence the terms adult education and the education of adults were distinguished, the latter referring to any form of education that occurs during adulthood. However, there is another way of interpreting the term 'adult education' that is more significant here. 'Adult' can be regarded here as an adjective, describing the type of education that occurs; a form of education that is adult in content, teaching and learning methods, relationships and in respect of the environment in which it occurs. Unfortunately, a lot of adult education does not conform to this high ideal, often because the facilities do not exist, but occasionally because those involved in the teaching and learning process still have expectations and impressions of education gained from their initial education in school.

Whether there should be such a difference between the education of children and that of adults is a moot point, but one that is beyond the scope of this book to debate in detail. Suffice it to note that if the process of education undergone by children denies their humanity then it may be that the learning process is not of an educational nature. However, such a distinction was drawn by Malcolm Knowles when he originally suggested that pedagogy referred to the education of children and andragogy to the education of adults. Even though he (1980) has recently withdrawn his claims for this exclusive distinction, it is worth focusing upon his formulation of andragogy within this context.

Andragogy, according to Knowles (1978: 55-9) is a theory based upon four major tenets that are different from pedagogy. They are:

(a) The Self-concept – the adult has a self-concept which requires that he should be perceived by others as being self-directing, so that when he finds himself in a position where this is not possible a tension is created between that situation and the self-concept of the learner.
(b) Experience – the adult brings to his learning the wide resources of his own experience and if that experience is devalued in the learning situation the learner feels that it is not merely his experience but he himself which is being rejected.
(c) Readiness to Learn – the adult is ready to learn those things that he perceives to be relevant to his situation.
(d) Orientation to Learning – the adult has a problem-centred orientation to learning.

Knowles has clearly propounded some significant ideas here, although they require thorough analysis. For example, implicit in these ideas is that of the adult as self-directing. This is a definition of adulthood which has more to do with maturity than with age and which is certainly debatable. Additionally, not all adults may have a problem-centred orientation to learning. Hence the theory is open to considerable discussion. Indeed, it could be argued that these four points, by which he tried to distinguish andragogy from pedagogy, require much more empirical evidence than he actually produced. However, the point of raising Knowles' work here is not to offer criticism but

to highlight the way in which he emphasises the significance of
the individual learner in the learning process - the self, the
individual's experience, the learner's perception of relevance
are all central to Knowles' thinking. Kidd (1973: 131), focusing
upon a similar set of ideas, suggested that perhaps 'the most
important task in learning is the development of a self that can
deal with reality'.

Education, then, is a learning process in which the learner,
not the subject being studied, is of most importance. Education
is about the learner - it is a process that has a humanistic basis.
It is, therefore, quite misleading to try to take the learner out
of the definition of education. Peters' third criterion, it will be
recalled, specified that the learner had to be willing and learning
voluntarily, but Peters may be too restrictive in trying to discuss the state in which the learner should be. Rather, it is
preferred to specify here that the educational process should
be one which is based upon the recognition of the humanity of
the participants.

This claim has certain implications that require some discussion.
It may be asked whether the process is still educational if the
participants learn what they were required to learn, even though
their humanity had not really been given the opportunity to
develop greatly during the process of learning. Clearly, if the
objectives of the exercise had been achieved, it might have been
satisfactory to the employing authority, who sponsors its
employees on the learning exercise. But the learners were then
means to other ends, which raises questions about the morality
of the process from the perspective of the employing authority.
Indeed, it is difficult to consider any learning process, in which
the humanity of the learners is not respected, as being morally
good. Consequently, it is suggested that education is a morally
good process in as much as the humanity of the participants is
respected and given opportunity to develop. Processes where
this does not happen are less than morally good and fall short
of the high ideals of education. It is this that fundamentally
constitutes the 'humanistic basis' referred to in the original ·
definition of education, although it must also be recognised that
many learning processes occur within the context of education
but which are not 'good' educational processes, because of the
inhibition and constraints experienced by the learner. Yet in
such processes the humanity of the learner theoretically might
have been considered and developed, so that they may be
classified as educational. Hence 'good' and 'bad' in this context
refer to the type of method employed in the learning process,
the forms of human interaction that occur in the process and
even the aims of the process itself. Education is a normative
process, there are high humanistic ideals implicit in the process
but perfection is rarely achieved, although failure to do so is
no excuse for not constantly trying.

Other processes, by contrast, do not allow for the humanity
of the participants to be liberated and developed. By the very

nature of the processes, restrictions and constraints are placed upon the participants and these processes are not recognised as being educational, even though learning may occur. Nevertheless, there may be occasions when these non-educational processes are employed for the good of the participants, so that they do not have to be always regarded as wrong. Yet when they are employed in this manner, they are not educational but something else. For instance, conditioning may be a learning process although it is not really educational. Yet when the learner is conditioned by the teacher some form of therapy may have occurred, but it would be quite incorrect to regard it as educational.

Hence, it is maintained that education is a normative process and that its value is to be located in the participants of the process. Where their humanity is respected and allowed to develop, then the process may be regarded as good but it is 'bad' if this does not occur. It is now necessary to examine some of these learning processes in order to relate them to this discussion.

LEARNING PROCESSES AND EDUCATIONAL PROCESSES

A learning process is one in which the participants acquire additional knowledge, new skills or changed attitudes as a result of undergoing the process - but not all learning processes are educational. Only those processes that conform to the criteria incorporated within the definition offered in the opening chapter are regarded as educational; that is, that they are a series of learning incidents, which are planned and which have a humanistic basis. It is possible, therefore, to list all the processes in which learning occurs and to decide upon whether, according to these three criteria, they are actually educational processes. Eleven such processes are mentioned here, but it is necessary to recognise that the mere listing of these processes in a written form itself reflects certain values and biases. It is, therefore, necessary to specify that, since learning is central to much of this discussion, the processes are described from the perspective of the learner.

In these processes learning occurs through: self-direction; facilitation; being taught; being instructed; being trained; discussion; living; being socialised; being influenced; being conditioned; being indoctrinated.

It will no doubt be noticed here that training occurs in this list but education does not. Yet the debate about education and training is one to which frequent reference is made and educators in the professions are well aware of the manner by which the preparation of professionals undergoes a change from 'training' to 'education' in terminology as the occupation professionalises. However, this may be more than merely a change in terminology to reflect a change in status, it may also reflect the fact that the occupation has begun to build its own body of knowledge that new recruits are expected to learn. Hence the term 'education' is incorporated into the preparation of the recruits to the occupation. Some new professions, such as teaching itself, have tended to drop the term 'training' totally and in this instance, 'teacher education' is now a more common expression. Other occupations, such as district nursing, have retained training and refer to the preparation of their new entrants as 'the education and training of . . .' Yet if education can refer to the acquisition of knowledge, skills or attitudes, the debate about education and training may be rather sterile, because training and education may not be 'likes' which may be compared. Since it has been suggested that professional education involves the acquisition of knowledge, skill and attitudes, it is considered unnecessary to enter this debate about the distinction between the two. Even so, it is necessary to examine briefly the eleven learning processes listed above in the context of professional education, so that each is now discussed in turn.

Self-directed Learning.   This form of learning occurs when the learner embarks upon a process of learning without the guidance of a teacher. Through reading, attending lectures, joining associations, attending conferences, etc., the learner pursues his own ends. Gross (1977: 24) records the story of Cornelius Hirschberg who 'learned that true liberal education can be achieved in the midst of the busiest adult life. He used the subway ride to and from work each day and his lunch hour.' He estimated that he had undertaken twenty thousand hours of serious reading during his working life exploring history, mathematics, the sciences, literature, music, art and philosophy. This is but one of a multitude of examples that could have been used to illustrate the lifelong, self-directed learner.

The significance of this form of learning for the professional is that it is this commitment to learning that enables him to keep abreast with recent developments in his own specialism. This is a manifestation of the ideology of professionalism - that the professional practitioner endeavours to use his spare moments in a process of self-directed learning, so that he can always provide the highest level of service to his clients.

Since there is no teacher, the learner's own self-motivation is significant, it is his own humanity that directs the process of development. Within self-directed learning the highest ideals of education may appear and through the learning process the learner may be enriched and developed.

Learning through Facilitation. Facilitation means 'to assist' or 'to enable something to occur' and this has become a most significant teaching method in adult education, especially in recent years. In this instance, the teacher is not the fount of all wisdom to whom the students turn, or at whose feet they sit. The teacher sees his role as an enabler, one who assists in the learning process, but not one who pontificates over it. Carl Rogers (1969: 157ff) has enumerated principles of learning and of facilitation that relate to this section. His principles of learning reflect ideas discussed earlier since they revolve around the significance of the self-concept of the learner and the learner's own motivation to learn. He recognises the role of the facilitator as one who can enable the learner to achieve his own aims while he, the educator, acts as a resource person. This approach to learning and teaching is foreign to many educators, since teachers have usually associated their role with transmitting knowledge rather than primarily helping the student to learn.

There have been a few experiments in professional education (e.g. Jones 1981) in which the teacher facilitates the learner's learning rather than offers instruction. Clearly this approach might initially be considered threatening by students who have never experienced this freedom, but if education is considered to be liberating then it should be liberating in methods as well as in the successful achievement of an end-product. Enabling the students to discover a degree of freedom in the learning process is, self-evidently, recognition of the learner's own humanity and, as such, this conforms to the highest ideals of the educational process.

It might be objected that for some learners this freedom is too traumatic for them to cope with and, therefore, it is only a respect for the humanity of the strong. Much initial education may have created dependent learners and, therefore, the facilitator who respects the humanity of the learners may be able to offer more support to those who need it until they are ready and able to achieve a greater degree of independence. While this could be accepted, it is no refutation of this approach to teaching and learning to suggest that there are some who might not be able to respond to the freedom to learn, since its manifest aim is to assist all to achieve a greater degree of freedom in learning with whatever assistance the learner might require.

Learning through Being Taught. Unlike facilitation, teaching implies that the teacher is much more involved in the process of helping the learner acquire knowledge because the teacher is actually teaching, i.e. transmitting knowledge. However, there is implicit in the term 'teaching' the idea of a relationship between the learner and the transmitter of knowledge or skill; the teacher is concerned to know that the learner has acquired that which the teacher transmitted. Hence, there is a definite concern about the methods employed in order to convey knowledge and skills, so that they may be learned more easily or more effectively.

Teaching is associated much more with initial education and perhaps adult liberal education than with further and higher education, which might be indicative of the relative status of the former. Since professional education has endeavoured to be associated with the latter, it might suggest that teaching is a

method of aiding the learner to acquire the requisite knowledge
rather than a combination of knowledge and skills that should
play a significant role in the education of recruits to the professions. However, high status does not necessarily imply 'good'
education, and it is sometimes agreed that teaching methods in
institutions of higher education may be inefficient. Teaching is
a process in which human interaction occurs and in which new
knowledge and skills are acquired. By virtue of the human interaction the learner may be in a position to question the ideas
with which he is presented and, consequently, to be able to
understand that which he learns.

Learning through Being Instructed. Unlike teaching, instruction
is a one-way process, from the expert to the one being initiated.
Knowledge and skill are presented, described, demonstrated and
once this has been undertaken the instructor's role has been
completed and the learner's has begun. This is the method of
the lecture and the demonstration; through it, much knowledge
is presented and skills demonstrated but whether they are
actually learned is another matter. Mannheim and Stewart (1962:
14) epitomise instruction thus: 'here is material which has been
sorted out to be presented to you. You should assess it - take
it or leave it.' Bligh (1971: 3), writing specifically about the
lecture, states:

> The lecturer's indispensability is not obvious from present
> evidence. Similarly, the lecture method is not economic in
> terms of time or anything else, if it cannot achieve its required
> objectives, and thus achievement is open to investigation. In
> the same way I am suspicious of lecturers who see virtue in
> 'covering more ground'. What is important is what the students
> learn, not how much the lecturer covers.

Thus, it may be seen that instruction may be an educational
process, but it need not be. It may take into consideration the
learner's previous knowledge or experience, it may take into
consideration the learner's humanity and it may result in learning or understanding. But it may not do any of these things.
However, its aim may always be to bring about learning and
understanding. Hence it may be argued that there is a place for
learning through instruction within educational processes, but
that this is not so self-evident as it may sometimes appear.

Learning through Being Trained. As occupations have pro-
fessionalised, so they have tended to substitute the term 'education' for 'training'. Training is a lower status. Additionally,
as they have generated a body of professional knowledge which
recruits should learn, consequently, education is regarded as
playing a more significant role. However, it was pointed out
above that the education versus training debate may be rather
sterile, so that it will not be rehearsed here. By contrast, it

will be argued that there is an important place for learning
through being trained in professional education but, before this
is done, it is necessary to explore the meanings and implications
of the term 'train'.

Collins English Dictionary' (1979: 1539) provides five meanings
of the word: to guide or teach; to control or guide towards a
specific goal; to do exercises and to prepare for a specific
purpose: to improve or curb by subjecting to discipline; to
focus or bring to bear. In education, training is usually
associated with a combination of these meanings. More specifically,
it is associated with either the physical fitness approach of the
third or to do exercise in order to improve the manipulative
techniques for a specific vocational purpose. Often the vocational
purpose is seen as a mindless repetition of procedures, performed at great speed, on a mass production line. Learning such
mindless procedures may not allow the process to be classified
as educational, even though sophisticated methods of teaching
skills have been developed in recent years - see Belbin and
Belbin (1972).

By contrast, in professional education, a relationship exists
between 'knowledge that', 'knowledge how' and skill which
indicates that in the professions learning a skill may be more
complicated than the mindless acquisition of psycho-motor
techniques. In this instance, it is a combination of knowledge
and skill that makes the application of the procedure a more
sophisticated and meaningful occupation and, as such, a much
more important exercise than it often appears to be from the
balance of theory and practice in professional education.

Training has also often been associated with an instruction-like
learning process whereby the trainer demonstrates the exercise
or skill and then leaves the learner to acquire the proficiency.
Yet Belbin and Belbin (1972) demonstrate that modern training
methods are much more akin to teaching with the trainer being
aware of various approaches to learning and also respecting the
humanity or individuality of the learner. In short, the trainer
may actually be a very skilled and knowledgeable teacher, so
that the acquisition of professional skills may be viewed as a
significant educational process. Even so, it must be recognised
that some training processes, such as doing physical exercise
under instruction in order to produce a greater level of physical
fitness, may not be educational.

Learning through Discussion. In one sense, the facilitator of
educational processes may create discussion groups through
which learning occurs. Yet there are incidents when learners
teach and learn by discussion between themselves. Clearly if
these discussion groups occur on an ad hoc basis without any
premeditation then they lack both the continuity and the intention of an educational process. Nevertheless, self-help groups
may be established without a teacher, but in which the learners
jointly plan their programme, so that they may achieve pre-

specified learning outcomes. It would be hard to deny that this form of self-help group, a form of self-directed learning, is anything other than an educational process.

Peters (1967: 21) suggests that conversation is a method in which the sharing of the experiences of each participant may result in considerable learning. Naturally, conversation is a method of learning but it may not be an educational process since it may lack both the continuity and the pre-specified aims of such a process. Nevertheless, conversation may be a method employed by a facilitator to stimulate awareness as part of an educational process.

Learning through Living. The human being has the capacity to reflect upon his experiences of everyday life and to learn from those experiences. This is being recognised in a number of American universities now, where credit is given for life experience when undertaking further education. However, it is doubtful whether it would be wise to regard living as an educational process because to do so would be to equate learning with education, something that was explicitly rejected in the opening chapter of this book. This is not to deny that much is learned by the individual merely by living, nor is it to deny that the term education is often employed to denote precisely this fact. However, it is recognised that while life may constitute a learning process for most individuals, it is not an educational one.

Learning through Being Socialised. Socialisation is a process discussed frequently by sociologists. Berger and Luckmann (1967) distinguish between primary and secondary socialisation: the former being that process which the individual undergoes in childhood, while the latter is any subsequent process that inducts the person into wider spheres in the objective world of reality. Socialisation itself is the process by which the objective world of reality is internalised and becomes subjectively meaningful. Clearly, during the process of being socialised into the wider society the individual learns a great deal, initially perhaps everything he learns. But as he grows older, socialisation may play a less significant part in learning. Even so, it is an important concept for educators in the professions, since socialisation into an occupation is a major part of secondary socialisation. This is so important that one sociologist, Musgrave (1967), has suggested that the process whereby the individual learns the role behaviour particular to his own occupation should be distinguished from secondary socialisation and regarded as a separate process which he calls tertiary socialisation. This socialisation process is an element of the hidden curriculum in professional education.

Whatever the merits of these sociological points it is significant here to recognise that during the process of professional education, a concurrent learning process is occurring - that of socialisation. Indeed, many of the learning experiences that the new recruit has during this period are as a result of socialisation. But is this learning experience an educational process?

It must be recalled that one of the elements in the definition of an educational process was that it is 'directed towards the participant(s)' learning and understanding', but this does not occur in socialisation. Much is learned and understood as a result of the human ability to reflect upon experiences but this is sometimes an unplanned and unintended outcome of the experience. Hence, it is maintained that although professional socialisation occurs concurrently with professional education, they are two distinct processes.

Learning through being Influenced. This process differs only slightly from the previous two, but it is dealt with separately because learners are frequently exposed to the values, biases and prejudices of their teachers. Since the learners are adults it is often accepted in the education of adults that the teacher is at liberty to express his own preferences. It would be surprising to expect anything else in a relationship between adults but the teacher does have a different status from that of the students, so that any expression of his opinion might underlie influence on the learners. Hence, they learn from the teacher and are influenced by him but this latter process is more akin to professional socialisation than to professional education.

Teachers should be aware that they are involved in concurrent processes and in each they play a different role; in the one they are educators of new recruits to the profession and in the other they may be a role model in professional socialisation. When students learn from the teachers in the sense of being influenced by them, then the process that has occurred is not really an educational one. Invariably the two processes are intertwined and it is difficult to separate them, but for the purpose of this analysis it is important that they should be seen as distinct processes.

Learning through Being Conditioned. Two types of conditioning occur: classical and operant. Classical conditioning is associated with Pavlov (1849-1936) who showed how dogs learned to associate the sound of a bell with the provision of food and, consequently, salivated at the sound of the bell. Subsequent research has shown how classical conditioning affects human behaviour and Lovell (1980: 35ff) points out that some adults study subjects because they have been conditioned to enjoy the subject by the warm, friendly atmosphere that a tutor creates. Teachers classically condition their students, whether they intend to or not, by the emotional climate they create in the learning environment.

Operant conditioning, however, is associated most frequently with B.F. Skinner, and some behaviourists have argued that all human learning can be interpreted in its terms. This form of conditioning is associated with reward and punishment and it is claimed that learners acquire the knowledge, skills and attitudes that they know from previous experience will evoke the most reward. Hence goals, rewards, incentives and even high marks are all rewards that act as positive reinforcements to learning. Unpleasant experiences act as negative reinforcers which will redirect or restimulate the learner. Once again it is clear that whether teachers intend to, or not, they condition their learners in an operant manner by virtue of their responses to students' learning experiences.

Thus it may be seen that conditioning is a phenomenon from which it is difficult to escape and that both forms are certainly aids to learning. Even so, these means may infringe one of the basic criteria of an educational process - they may not have a humanistic basis. However humanely the teacher employs these techniques he may be manipulating, and consequently dehuman- ising, the learner to some extent. But, it may be argued, what if the professional teacher manipulates the learner by employing these techniques for the learner's own good? What if the learner was enabled to pass his professional examinations only because the teacher used these techniques on him? Surely in this instance it may be considered beneficial to the student? These points may all be true but it still does not make conditioning an educational process. It does make it a technique that can produce more efficient learning in a student but this is still not the same as an educational process. Yet, conditioning techniques may be employed in such a way as to enhance the dignity of the learner and then it may be regarded as a teaching technique in an edu- cational process.

From the above discussion it may be recognised that condition- ing occurs in educational processes, as it does in other processes of living. Yet there are certain dangers in employing these techniques. For instance, the learner is being manipulated and this is lessening his independence and his humanity; the learner may be being encouraged to learn but not necessarily become critically aware of what is being learned; the learner is being encouraged to learn for reasons that, while perfectly under- standable, may not be sufficient for a professional. This last point might need some explanation. The professional must have knowledge, even if he does not employ it immediately, so that he must learn it even if there is no overt reward for acquiring it. A doctor, for instance, may learn about some rare disease or obscure technique but never meet the disease or never use the skill, so that no reward for having learned it may ever be forth- coming. Yet he may need it, because he may meet that rare case and then his professionalism will be put to use to the service of his patient and the sense of satisfaction gained, and the praise or thanks offered may reinforce him to continue to keep abreast with developments in his profession. Hence the professional should be expected to learn without the reinforcements that ensue as a result of being able to use what is acquired. Naturally, it could be argued that he might have been conditioned into learning this knowledge and skill in any case, so that the argument is not valid.

Obviously in the very process of living every individual will probably be conditioned to some extent but to employ these techniques deliberately may be to lessen any educational process and dehumanise the learner. Hence, it is argued here that whatever the effects of conditioning, the processes are not in themselves educational ones even though they may be used in the facilitation of learning.

Learning through Being Indoctrinated. The word means 'to teach (a person or group of people) systematically to accept doctines, especially uncritically . . . (or rarely) to impart learning to; instruct . . .' ('Collins English Dictionary' 1979: 746ff). Clearly it is the first of these two meanings that is most frequently employed in education, and which is most often labelled as being 'bad' or 'wrong' in some manner.

The previous discussion on conditioning overlapped with the idea of indoctrination since it was suggested that certain techniques might be employed in order to bring about desired learning outcomes in the learners. This implies that teaching methods might be one facet of indoctrination and Crittenden (1972: 146) concurs with this, when he suggests that indoctrination occurs:

> If a teacher uses any pedagogical method in the presentation of the specified content which is inconsistent with the requirements of the general nature of enquiry and moral principles, assuming that intellectual and emotional development of his students is taken into account.

Crittenden, however, disputes Hare's (1964) claim that one of the major differences between education and indoctrination lies in the aims of the teacher. He suggests that Hare's position may be better understood in respect of the content of the teaching rather than the aims but since the content is largely determined by the aims, Crittenden's position is not entirely convincing. It is, therefore, necessary to examine the aims of professional education in relation to this discussion. Since indoctrination refers to beliefs, the main area in which it may be argued that indoctrination might occur in professional education lies in that of professionalism. If the teacher seeks to produce students who all hold beliefs about professional practice similar to his own, then he embarks upon the teaching and learning process with the intention of indoctrinating them. By contrast if he intends students to examine the ideology, so that they can construct their own ideologies, he intends to educate them. Therefore, it is maintained that in respect of aims, indoctrination and education are totally opposed. Education seeks to free the learner's mind whilst indoctrination aims to bind it. The aim that a teacher has may determine the method he employs to teach an ideology, but this may also affect the content being taught. But before this is discussed, it is necessary to note how close this discussion on aims has come to behavioural objectives. Davies (1976: 14ff) states that specific 'objectives attempt to describe, in the clearest possible terms, exactly what a student will think, act or feel at the end of a learning experience'. While the educational process has overall aims in terms of learning and understanding it appears that behavioural objectives actually approach the position where they could be classified as intended indoctrination and, therefore, the morality of the use of behavioural objectives becomes questionable.

It is now necessary to examine the contention that the content taught may provide a basis for indoctrination. Crittenden (1972: 146) claims that:

> If a teacher presents the specified content in such a way that he violates the criteria of inquiry - unwarranted claims, suppression of critical evaluation or reasons and evidence, etc.

but that 'it should not be assumed that any teaching of content . . . is ipso facto indoctrination'. Hence Crittenden is claiming that it is how the teacher treats the content rather than the content itself that is indoctrinational. Since one of the aims of education is to help students to develop a critical awareness of what they are taught it seems that the content of the teaching is less significant in indoctrination, among adult students especially, since the learners are able to reject it, provided that they are not intimidated by the authority or status of the teacher.

Thus, it is suggested here that indoctrination may occur in the intention and in the method rather than in the content of what is taught. In both aim and method in the process of indoctrination, the learner's humanity is not respected nor is he encouraged to develop a critical understanding of the content with which he is presented. Indoctrination, therefore, is a learning process, but it is not one that may be classified as educational.

Eleven learning processes have been examined briefly in this section, some of them may be regarded as educational processes but some of the latter ones are certainly not. Some of these do not respect the humanity of the learners and may be regarded as undesirable forms of learning. Among the learning processes that are educational are: self-directed learning, learning through facilitation, learning through being taught, learning through instruction, learning through training and learning through discussion. Even so, some of these processes do not always attain the high ideals of education and when this occurs the process may be classified as 'bad' education and the moral phraseology reflects that in these instances it is sometimes the learner's humanity that is in some way put at risk. Hence it may be seen that through this argument value is placed upon persons rather than processes or content and it is for this reason that education is regarded as a learning process having a humanistic basis.

LEARNING AND TEACHING

Throughout the previous section on learning processes the theme of teaching has constantly recurred, so that it is now appropriate that the topic of teaching should be analysed. Teaching may be defined as an activity intended to help the participants acquire learning and understanding and, from the above discussion, it may be seen that since teaching demands human interaction with the learners it contains a significant moral dimension. As the previous section demonstrated, some teaching activities preclude the teaching and learning process from being classified as educational and, therefore, at the heart of teaching in education is a respect for persons. This claim is as true for the education of children as it is in the education of adults. Yet it is also evident from the above discussion that not all teaching has the same approach and Scheffler (1973) has suggested three philosophical models of teaching that have significance here: the impression model, the intuition model and the rule model. Each of these is now briefly analysed.

The Impression Model

Scheffler actually presents two versions of this model, one based upon sense experience and the other upon the learner being the recipient of verbal information. In both instances there is an underlying behaviourist perspective which assumes that the learner, being the recipient of information, will store it and as the body of knowledge expands so the learner will be presented with an increasing amount of information. Such teaching and learning methods as instruction and training, as well as conditioning, reflect these ideas. The strength of this position is that it demonstrates that to some extent the mind is a function of its experience but such an approach to teaching precludes an explanation of the way by which the learner is able to use that knowledge and even to innovate upon it, nor does it actually encourage the learner to do this.

The Insight Model

This approach to teaching suggests that the mind does not only store the sense impressions gained in the teaching and learning situation but that knowledge is fundamentally based upon understanding, so that the teacher's words, etc. are merely a means by which the learner seeks to make sense of some element of the objectified body of knowledge. Having received a sense of meaning the learner is then able to apply it to specific situations. Hence the teacher who adopts this approach should help the learner to understand the underlying meaning, rather than just the information that may be stored in the mind. This is certainly an improvement on the previous model, but it is not without its weaknesses. In the first instance, knowledge is more than insight into meaning, so that it does not really help the learner to analyse, synthesise or to evaluate that knowledge. Nor does the approach enable the learner to understand the principles and reasons associated with evaluating such knowledge, so that while the model has more to offer than the impression one it does not provide a philosophical model of teaching that reflects the high ideals of education suggested in the initial discussion.

The Rule Model

In this approach, Scheffler suggests that the learner needs to be able to evaluate knowledge in a reasonable manner. Hence, underlying teaching should be a set of principles based upon reason, so that knowledge is both presented and evaluated in a rational way. For Scheffler, principles, reasons and consistency combine in rationality, which is an essential attribute of human dignity. He argues that education should seek to develop in people a character that is principled in thought and action and in which the dignity of the human being is manifest. Hence teaching should be designed to introduce students to those principles that underlie the conception of rationality and which the teachers themselves should acknowledge as fundamental, general and impartial to thought and action.

While there are some strengths in all three perspectives and it is important that students entering the professions store factual knowledge and understand meanings, it is also essential that they develop that sense of rationality as is indicated in the 'rule model', so that this constitutes a useful philosophical model for teaching. This analysis in no way determines the methods or techniques that a teacher should employ, discussion of which is beyond the scope of this study, but it does offer an underlying rationale for teaching that is in accord with the general understanding of all the forms of education discussed here.

CONCLUSION

Many types of learning process occur during professional education and new recruits to the ranks of the professions should acquire knowledge, skills and attitudes appropriate to their professional practice during their training. That knowledge may be something that they internalise at the level of storing facts and information, but then it may be very important for a professional practitioner to be aware of specific facts and information.

Additionally, the learner should acquire the ability to apply that knowledge since a knowledgeable practitioner who is unable to apply that knowledge is little better than a practical person who has no knowledge to apply. Yet it is essential for the practitioner to have the ability to assess the information and facts with which he is presented, since unless he is able to do this he will be in no position to introduce new innovations into practice with safety. The question needs to be raised about the level of knowledge that a profession expects of its new recruits. Indeed, is safety to practice a matter of possessing the knowledge and being able to apply it to the level required? Alternatively, is it the ability to evaluate the validity and relevance of new knowledge and to apply it in specific situations? Questions such as this demand that the relationship between the levels of knowledge expected and the means by which that knowledge is acquired should be carefully worked out by educators in the professions. However, it is not merely a matter of learning and teaching, professions have to examine and assess a new recruit's competency to enter practice, so that the following chapter concentrates on appraisal in professional education.

The terms examination, assessment and evaluation are all employed in education to refer to different forms of appraisal. All of the terms are used in the education of professionals, so that it is important that the foundations of appraisal in education are considered. Nevertheless, it must be borne in mind that education alists have developed many sophisticated techniques for testing students, that a considerable amount of research has been conducted and the published literature on this subject is voluminous. While reference will be made to some of it, the aim of this chapter is to explore some of the important questions that underlie the whole of the examination procedure.

It is rather difficult to distinguish conceptually between the three terms employed in the previous paragraph and, for the sake of convenience, conventional education usage will be retained here. Hence 'evaluation' will be employed specifically in relation to the curriculum while the other two terms will refer to testing students. 'Examination' will be used in relation to the more formal kind of appraisal, usually end-of-course, end-of-term, etc., of a summative nature, while 'assessment' will be employed to refer to the formative type of procedures that occur throughout the educational process and to informal written tests used occasionally in education.

The process of appraisal itself usually refers to the attempt to measure competency or to test the level of knowledge, etc. possessed by a person. In many instances it involves more than an objective measure of factual knowledge and includes placing a value upon a piece of work or assessing the extent to which a student or practitioner is competent to practise. This demands some discussion about the concepts of competency and standards. Yet even before this is undertaken it is necessary to explore the reasons why any form of examination is regarded as necessary in education and, then, to decide whether the values required in making these assessments are objective or subjective. Thereafter, the concepts of competency and standards are discussed. Subsequently, the relationship between competency and the aims of professional education are explored and this leads to an analysis of the criteria for examinations. Finally, there is a brief discussion about curriculum evaluation.

TOWARDS A RATIONALE FOR APPRAISAL

It is important in professional education that assessment procedures are not adopted merely because they are utilised in a
prestigious educational institution, i.e. a university, or in a
high-status profession. Indeed, it is necessary to enquire
whether appraisal is even necessary in professional education
or whether education would be just as efficient without having
any system of appraisal. It will facilitate the discussion if the
reasons suggested by one educationalist are employed as a basis
for this.

Rowntree (1977: 15ff) suggests six reasons for appraising
students: selection, maintaining standards, motivating students,
providing feedback to students, providing feedback to teachers,
preparation for life. Since this list is quite comprehensive, no
attempt is made here to add to it and each reason will be discussed in turn.

Many educators in the professions are involved, at one stage
or another, in selecting candidates for the courses that they
organise. Often this process also results in selecting the recruits
for the profession itself. Hence an education department lecturer,
interviewing candidates for a course in education, may also be
selecting recruits to teaching. By contrast, a district nurse
tutor interviewing candidates may only be selecting them for the
course, already knowing that the management have found them
acceptable as potential employees. Whatever the actual procedures
for selection for the profession and its training, the processes
are often hidden in a shroud of secrecy. Successful applicants
to the course know that they have a place but the remainder
usually receive a communication informing them that there is no
place for them. This procedure, where it occurs, requires consideration. If educators regard the selection interview as a learning situation for all the participants and if they regard education
as a humanistic process, they may be denying their own philosophy if they do not help unsuccessful candidates to learn more
from the interview than the fact that they have not been
accepted. Indeed, it might be argued that it is immoral not to
help unsuccessful candidates to do better in their next interview. By contrast, it might be argued that the interview is not
regarded as part of the educational process and, that since
interviewing itself is rather subjective, it is not expedient to
expose the lack of objectivity in the selection process to the
unsuccessful candidates. If the discussion is removed from the
sphere of education and placed within the context of human
interaction, it is possible to argue that not imparting useful
information to one of the participants in the process is itself
immoral, since it is a failure to help another person who should
have a right to learn.

Frequently the professions stipulate criteria prior to entry and
often included in these is a minimum level of educational achievement, e.g. five GCE 'O' level passes, two 'A' level passes and

the possession of a degree awarded by a university or the
Council for National Academic Awards. It is sometimes claimed
that these qualifications are necessary to show that a candidate
can cope with the rigours of the course of study, but Jarvis and
Gibson (1981) have cast doubts on this in respect of district
nurse education and Rowntree (1977: 17ff) suggests that 'medicaı
students with poorer entry qualifications but with concern and
empathy for ordinary people may emerge as better general
practitioners than academic high flyers who may feel that they
have failed if they do not get to be specialists or researchers'.
Hence it is necessary to ask why the professions actually stipulate academic entry qualifications, rather than motivational and
personality prerequisites. More important, from the perspective
of professional education, it is necessary to recognise that there
is no logical connection between, for instance, the ability to pass
GCE 'O' level history and the ability to nurse a sick patient or
to design a building. Hence there appear to be no educational
reasons why this form of educational achievement should be
stipulated as a prerequisite for entry into a profession. By
contrast, it might be argued that there is a necessary and
logical connection between a demonstrated level of competence
in mathematics, for instance, and the ability to cope with an
engineering course which assumes a specific level of mathematics
as a starting point for training. In this case, demonstration of
competency in a discipline is a logical criterion for selection.
Basically the two positions illustrated here may be characterised
thus: the first suggests that because an individual can do 'a',
or 'a + b' etc. he can necessarily do 'x', but the second suggests
that because an individual succeeds in 'a' he is likely to continue
to achieve success in 'a' if he is given the opportunity. Hence,
the second approach to selection, placing emphasis upon continuity in educational progression, has the merit of being logical.
   Nevertheless, such an approach also has a number of weaknesses, requiring consideration. Many professions make their
initial selection of recruits at either the university entrance stage
or immediately following completion of the university degree.
Expectation that new entrants should have achieved a level of
competency in one of the academic disciplines upon which a profession is based may prevent a recruit from studying a wide
range of subjects in initial education prior to work preparation.
This may occur because, in order to achieve that level of competency, early intellectual specialisation may have occurred.
This may result in some individuals being ignorant of other
forms of knowledge and thus they are impoverished in this respect. It will be recalled that Pellegrino (1977) lamented the fact
that those who studied medicine were rarely also able to study
the humanities. Yet an alternative to early specialisation in
initial education is the prolongation of professional basic education. Curtailment of the actual length of the working life may
not be a phenomenon to be discouraged but the expense of
maintaining the lifelong full-time student might be too great for

most societies in the world to bear. This suggests that some system of recurrent education might be more beneficial and that professions should both encourage candidates to have a wide range of intellectual experiences prior to entry and also allow practitioners sabbatical leave in order to extend the breadth of their education thereafter. The former of these two suggestions might result in candidates to a profession being a little older on entry and, in this instance, it might be legitimate to stipulate specific broad academic prerequisites prior to entering professional education. However, it would then be necessary for educators and other professional practitioners to recognise that the reason for the demand of these entry prerequisites is breadth, rather than regarding them as evidence that the candidates might be able to cope with the course of study for which they had applied.

The whole of the educational process, including its assessment procedures, may also act as another selection mechanism for entry into the profession. The final, formal examinations may be the last hurdle to be surmounted prior to gaining access to the professional community. Failure, or referral, may delay entry until sufficient knowledge or skill has been gained to negotiate this final barrier successfully.

Yet it must be recognised that the standards achieved in examinations may merely reflect the examiner's assessment of the work produced for the examination itself. It may not be any guide to the standard of professional practice that a successful candidate will achieve thereafter. Yet the examination acts as both a tool of assessment in relation to the educational process and an entry gate into the profession. Unless the content of the curriculum of the educational process bears a close relationship to the demands of professional practice there may be little logical reason for allowing or preventing entry to the profession on the grounds of results gained in examinations.

Rowntree's (1977) second reason for appraisal is that it is necessary to maintain standards and this raises a very similar type of argument to that entered into in the discussion about professional competency in the third chapter, so that none of those points will be repeated here. End-of-course examinations, it might be argued, are necessary to test the competency of the students at about the time they are to enter professional practice. Yet the published research on the subject tends to suggest that there is little correlation between the grades awarded in professional education and achievement in professional practice (Hudson 1966; Berg 1973; Taylor et al. 1965). This might occur because there is little correlation between the course of professional education and the demands of professional practice, or because the method of examination is artificial. However, it is a research finding that requires more consideration than it has hitherto received in the education of some professionals.

Additionally, a number of other problems surround the assertion that appraisal is necessary in order to maintain standards.

Standards themselves vary between educational institutions, so that entrants to a profession may reflect the standard of their training rather than a standard required by the profession on entry to it. Different professions also have different methods of testing recruits: in some, the profession sets a national examination, for example the Law Society, while in others, the local examinations set by a university or polytechnic are accepted by the profession. In some training, assessment is made by use of course work assignments, in others, it depends on an end-of-course examination, while still other professions employ all three modes of assessment mentioned in this chapter, i.e. course work, examination and practical work. Again in some professions a pass mark is specified while in others only a quota of candidates are accepted for entry on to the professional register. Thus it may be seen that there is no standardisation of procedures for entry into the professions. Yet standardisation and the maintenance of standards are not synonymous and the problems of standardisation will be discussed later in this chapter. In regard to the maintenance of standards, it might be argued that whatever the form or procedure of appraisal, a method of quality control is introduced ensuring that those entering the profession have achieved a certain minimum level of competence. However, this assumption is one that cannot be taken for granted since it has already been argued that there may be no relation between examination grades and professional achievement. And since the ideological quality of professionalism rarely appears to be tested, it might be that the examinations, etc. are not actually testing that aspect of professional practice that is important to ensure continued competency.

Examinations may, however, act as an external motivation to students to study so that they might be successful in the assessment procedure and, thereby, enter the profession. However, if students require extrinsic factors to motivate them to study it might be wondered whether they will have the necessary motivation to continue studying during their professional career in order to render the highest possible quality of service to their clients. Nevertheless, assessment procedures may act as an external motivating force and yet still fail to assess the actual ability that they seek to ascertain. The whole process of examinations may so worry the adult, for instance, that the mature student does not do his own ability justice under examination conditions. Belbin and Belbin (1972: 167-9) record how adults in non-professional training have such a fear of examinations that some, in in-service education, resign from their job rather than undergo an examination which they might fail. While people in the professions may have a far more successful history in examinations, it would be quite illogical to suppose that these findings might not be relevant in some instances to professional examinations. Yet it might be argued that since life itself contains a number of hurdles that have to be negotiated, examinations are merely part of this preparation. Rowntree (1977: 29) disputes this claim on the grounds that most professions do not demand an ongoing series of examinations, so that this does not offer a logical defence of the examination system.

Some forms of assessment may be employed to provide feedback to both students and teachers of the students' learning and where the teacher might provide additional support. In this instance, appraisal may be viewed as a necessary part of the educational process since it enables the teaching and learning process to be pitched at the point of deficiency. Nevertheless, the extent to which examinations actually select the most appropriate candidates for the profession, examine or maintain standards or act as motivating agencies for students remains a little unclear. Before any of these questions are pursued further it is necessary to enquire whether the assessment undertaken is actually an objective phenomenon.

OBJECTIVE OR SUBJECTIVE VALUE: ASSESSING AND GRADING

Placing a mark upon a piece of work appears to give a degree of value to the work. It also appears to take on a level of objectivity. Yet this can be a misleading process and much depends upon the piece of work being marked. In some subjects, such as elementary mathematics, there are correct and incorrect answers and right and wrong ways of tackling the problems set. A script marker in this instance may mark the work and append a grade, say ten out of ten, or 100 per cent. In this instance the grade reflects an empirical reality and in the process of marking no evaluation has occurred. When the script marker reports that the paper that he has just marked has achieved a grade of 100 per cent and is, in his opinion, a good pass standard then an evaluation has occurred. Naturally, it would appear quite illogical for the script marker to state that he has just awarded a mark of 100 per cent and, in his opinion, the paper was of a poor standard. But what of a paper to which he had awarded 45 per cent, when 45 per cent was the pass mark? Is it a good paper, a poor paper or what? His assessment of the paper as poor might be because all the others had achieved a lot more marks! The reverse might have been true and the script marker claim that it was a satisfactory paper. Hence in these examples, the evaluation depends upon the script marker whereas the grade depends upon the degree of 'correctness' to the mathematical questions set. When factual knowledge is being tested, e.g. dosages in medicine, legal rulings, etc., it is possible to grade examinations in an objective manner, but where the knowledge is not factual then even the grade may be an evaluation.

There are different levels of knowledge besides factual recall, including understanding, evaluating, synthesising, analysing and applying (Bloom 1956), and many of these demand more than a simple application of a fact to an empirical situation resulting in a correct or an incorrect solution. Indeed, a variety of inter-

pretations may exist to a given question and a multitude of
different essays can be written on an open-ended question.
Greater difficulty exists when a supervisor is assessing practical
work, e.g. a field work teacher assessing a health visitor
student might not like the student's approach to the family and
give her a poor grade, even though the family actually benefited
by the student's innovative approach. Similar problems occur in
viva voce examinations. No simple method exists for assessing
the student: the subjectivity of the assessor comes to the fore.
Many attempts have been made in marking and assessing to overcome the subjective element in marking but ultimately these
forms of assessing and evaluating involve the human element.
Often, even in the types of assessment where the human element
has been operative, there are also objective elements that need
to be highlighted, for example an essay about nursing may contain incorrect factual data about drugs, so that in this instance
the overall grade awarded is a mixture of the subjective and the
objective. In most essays, the rules of logic might also form a
basis for objective assessment.

Yet when the subjective element is recognised, a final grade,
e.g. 65 per cent, or B, is awarded and this gives the appearance of objectivity, even though it actually reflects the personal subjective assessment of the examiner, or a mixture of the
objective and the subjective. Even when two examiners, an
internal and an external, agree on grades, this merely reflects
that the two examiners have roughly the same standards in
relation to the piece of work being assessed and that this
standard may be harsh or lenient (rather than that the piece
of work is objectively of a certain standard).

Hence, it is argued here, that with the exception of the
examination of empirically testable knowledge, the majority of
grades awarded in the educational process reflect the subjective
standards of the marker and the assessor. Indeed, value does
not lie in the phenomenon or the process but in the participants
or the recipients of the process. Value is a human quality and
spurious objectivity may be a disservice to the humanistic basis
of the educational process. This is not to deny that there are
standards, merely to demonstrate that those standards of practice are themselves learned, relative and subjective. They may
reflect the professionalism of the marker as much as the competency of the student, but the award grades may give a
spurious objectivity to a process that is largely subjective.

COMPETENCY AND STANDARDS

Standards may refer to 'a degree of excellence' or 'an average
quality' among other of its meanings. 'An average quality'
may not be a very meaningful phrase since 'average' may be a
high level of excellence if all the members are superb practitioners, whereas it may connote a poor level if all the prac-

titioners have been failed or referred already. Hence the term may be useful in everyday speech but not very meaningful in the context of this discussion, except that it implies the subjectivity and relativity of values. Within the framework of the present discussion the term 'standards' denotes 'a degree of excellence'. This is similar to the implication in the term 'professional' - that a high degree of excellence exists in the performance of an occupation. Yet if the value is of a subjective and relative nature, it may be asked who assesses the level excellence manifest in the practice? Traditionally, members of professions have always claimed that only fellow professionals are equipped to recognise the standard of professional practice that they observe. Indeed, Hall (1969: 82) suggested that among the attitudinal attributes of professionalisation is:

> Belief in self-regulation. This involves the belief that, since the persons best qualified to judge the work of the professional are his fellow professionals, colleague control is both desirable and practicable.

Leaving aside a number of points implicit in this statement, it may be seen that peer assessment is claimed to be a mark of professional practice. Nevertheless, it may be as important for the professional to be able to undertake a rigorous self-assesment of his practice. Inability to be self-aware may well result in poor standards of practice occurring without recognising it, since the clients may not be in a position to judge the professional expertise of the practitioner. It will be recalled that Hughes (1958) referred to the professional practitioner who could satisfy his clients but not his peers as a 'quack'. Yet the practitioner who is unable to satisfy his clients may not be a good practitioner either, since many clients are discerning and are aware of the service that they seek from the professional. Hence, it may be a mistake to dismiss the client's perspective as irrelevant. Thus it is claimed that standards in professional practice refer to a degree of excellence as adjudged by the practitioner, his peers and his clients.

Two terms have appeared in the above paragraph that require a brief explanation: peer assessment and self-assessment. Peer assessment refers to a mode of appraisal which is undertaken by individuals of the same rank or status as the person being assessed. It is important to recognise that the individuals undertaking this exercise are actually peers since the standards upon which the judgements are made may vary considerably with the expertise of the assessors. Nevertheless, this form of assessment has traditionally been one of the marks of a professional and, therefore, it is one that students in professional education should be encouraged to undertake. Self-assessment is an even more important skill to develop since many practitioners may rarely have their professional performance appraised overtly once they have finished their basic professional education.

Hence, students should be encouraged to be critical of themselves during that initial period, perhaps with the help of a supervisor or personal tutor, so that they may thereafter continue to assess their own performance in order to remain competent in practice. Thus, self-assessment in the presence of the tutor may serve as a useful teaching tool to help the student obtain a sense of high standards.

Competency itself is a concept that requires some brief elaboration. It refers to the fact that a candidate or a practitioner is adjudged to have achieved a level of excellence in practice acceptable to those fellow professionals who make the assessment. Once again it must be clearly noted that this is a subjective judgement, even though phrases like 'a level of excellence' suggest that there is an objective fixed standard that must be reached before approval is given.

It is important to recognise, therefore, that in professional education it is not only the grades in the written work that are a reflection of a subjective set of standards; assessment of practical competency also depends upon the values of the assessor. If high standards of excellence are to be achieved as a result of basic professional education then both the teachers and the assessors should hold those standards themselves in order to encourage their students to achieve them. Furthermore, by teaching self-assessment in practice, professional educators might help to ensure that those entering professional practice will continue to maintain high standards of excellence.

COMPETENCY AND THE AIMS OF PROFESSIONAL EDUCATION

In the third chapter the relationship between competency and the aims of professional education was explored in considerable detail and it is not the intention to repeat that here. Suffice to recall that it was suggested that professional education could not ensure that students would be competent practitioners for life, only that it should prepare them to have a professional ideology, sufficient knowledge and skills to enter practice and a critical understanding of the knowledge and skills that they had learned. Thus it seems logical to argue that prior to declaring a candidate for a profession competent to practise, he should have satisfied designated representatives of that profession that these three aims have been successfully achieved.

Traditionally, the knowledge upon which professional practice is based and a critical understanding of that knowledge has formed the basis of the written examination. However, there is often disjuncture between the theory and the practice. Wilson (1965) argued, for instance, that clergy fulfilled many practical roles for which their education and training had not prepared them, since they had been educated in theology but were frequently undertaking the role of social worker. Hence, a competent theologian might not be a competent clergyman! Thus it is important to ensure that the demands of practice form one of the bases for selection of the curriculum knowledge content which may then be assessed during and, perhaps, at the termination of initial professional education. Competency in practice seems to assume a lesser place in the hierarchy of assessment procedures in the professions, with many hardly including it at all. For instance, teachers in further and higher education do not have to have demonstrated competency in teaching before they are employed. This reflects the traditional pre-eminence ascribed to theoretical knowledge in education and in the professions, but that will be questioned in the final chapter. The first of the aims of professional education suggested earlier, that of helping students to acquire a professional ideology, is rarely tested overtly during initial training. This is hardly surprising, since it is difficult to give even the semblance of objectivity to testing these attitudes. Nevertheless, throughout the period of initial preparation, both during theory and practice, students' attitudes are being moulded and it is perhaps more important that a profession should satisfy itself that those whom it admits to its ranks ascribe to the ideals of professionalism. While the Hippocratic Oath in medicine can not ensure that doctors will continue to be fully competent throughout the whole period of their practice, it at least places the ideal of professionalism at the forefront of practice.

It has been argued thus far that since standards are subjective, ascriptions of competency to practise are themselves reflections of the standards of those who make them. Assessors are representatives of the profession, having the responsibility delegated to them, to test the level of knowledge, degree of skill and the professional attitudes of those seeking to gain admission to the professional community. Competency to enter practice, in the opinion of those who make the appraisal, is the only judgement that they can make. No guarantee exists that those who commence practice will remain competent, since knowledge and techniques change rapidly. Nevertheless, those who have the ability to recognise high standards and who seek to provide anything less than the best are those whose competency is more likely to be enduring, even though attitudes and commitment may be changed through time and by experiences in practice. It is for this reason that it is now being questioned as to whether those entering a profession should automatically be members of that profession for life or whether the credentials should be only for a limited period of time (see the discussion in Kreitlow et al. 1981: 45-70). Additionally, some professions are now introducing additional credentials that demonstrate that the practitioner has been appraised by his peers as having continued to acquire additional knowledge and expertise relevant to his practice. For instance, Houle (1980: 234) records how the American Medical Association makes Physician Recognition Awards to those who spend time furthering their professional education. These awards expire after a period of three years, so that it is essential for a practitioner who wishes to display his additional qualifications to continue his own education. In this way the profession is able to motivate some of its members to continue to keep abreast with latest developments and who may so retain a level of competency or even develop a higher one.

CRITERIA FOR EXAMINATIONS

It has been argued that nearly every form of appraisal is subjective and it is now necessary to isolate a number of criteria for examinations. It is suggested that examinations should: test what has been studied; test what they claim to test; test what is relevant to the professional practice; give an equal chance to all candidates to satisfy the examiners; be replicable; be fair. Each of these six basic criteria is now discussed.

Examinations Should Test What Has Been Studied

This seems to be a logical statement to make about examinations but it is possible for a profession to publish an outline curriculum for professional basic training and allow individual teaching centres to interpret it according to local demands, but still set a national paper. In this instance, there is a possibility that the selection of questions in the national paper omits all the areas that have been studied in depth in one or more of the teaching centres. While this is only hypothetical, once a profession has allowed flexibility in subject content in basic education the possibility exists that a national examination will not test those areas that have been studied. Hence, the logical outcome of allowing flexibility in the content of the curriculum is to allow the same type of flexibility in the assessment procedures, or else the examination may act as a restraint upon the original flexibility. However, it might be objected that allowing local examinations will result in teaching establishments limiting the breadth of the examination to those areas upon which they have concentrated, and that the total demands of professional practice will not actually be considered. This is a definite possibility, but in the original validation of the course the breadth of content to be included would have been agreed between the representatives of the profession and the educational institutions, so that the ethics of the contract obtain thereafter. Additionally, the profession should have the right to monitor local examinations in order to ensure that the content of the mutually agreed curriculum is taught and examined.

Examinations Should Test What They Claim to Test

If an examination seeks to test the candidate's knowledge and understanding of a professional academic discipline or the candidate's level of skill in professional practice then the exam-

inations should be designed so that these aims are actually
achieved. However, it is a well known complaint of the essay
type examination that it actually tests the essay writing skills
of the candidates as much as it tests their knowledge and
understanding. Examinations having a time limit give an advan-
tage to the candidate who can write fast and neatly. Oral examinations, another approach to appraisal, favour those who
interview well. Criticisms of the examination system are multi-
tudinous and, in addition, research has demonstrated that
many of these criticisms are justified (Mehrens and Lehmann
1978). Hence, it is necessary to define the aims of the test and
to select appropriate measures to achieve them and this may
call for innovation in examinations. Gibson and Jarvis (1982)
record how the new district nurse examination paper has been
restructured in order to test a number of different levels of
knowledge. Medicine and other professions have also experi-
mented with different forms of examination in order to test more
precisely those areas of knowledge that they claim to examine.

Examinations Should Test What Is Relevant to Professional Practice

Earlier in this chapter it was pointed out that the content of
clergy training did not relate to the actual demands of practice.
However, the demands of practice should constitute one of the
criteria for the selection of curriculum content. Additionally, it
was claimed earlier that the basis of professional competency
consists of a number of different areas of knowledge, specific
skills and a cluster of attitudes that relate to professional practice. If this case is broadly accepted, then it is incumbent upon
the profession to ensure that all of these aspects are examined
during professional basic education and that the candidates have
satisfied representatives of the profession in these areas. It is
illogical to examine candidates in one, or two, of these categories
without also testing them in the wider range of areas on which
professional competency may be based.

Candidates Should Have an Equal Chance to Satisfy the Examiners

It was pointed out that where a profession has a national examination, there is a certain degree of chance as to whether a
specific teaching centre has prepared its students to answer an
unseen paper as well as students from another centre. Yet there
exists a degree of luck in any unseen paper since some candidates
may have studied areas that are questioned in a paper whilst
other, even more brilliant, students, may have studied none of
the areas examined and subsequently gain lower grades. But it
might be argued that in the first instance the teaching centre
was at fault through not adequately preparing its students
whilst, in the second, students not revising the whole course
take a calculated risk, so that in neither case is it the fault of

the examination system. It might be conceded in the latter
instance that it was the fault of the students and in the former
the responsibility lies with the academic staff. Yet given the
constraints of time and the special demands of local areas or
individual interests there is still a risk that candidates might
not have an equal chance to demonstrate their competency to
the designated representatives of the profession. However, it
may be possible to lessen this potential inequality by redevising
the methods of testing rather than by not seeking to appraise
at all.

The Results of an Examination Should Be Replicable

In a now famous piece of research, Hartog and Rhodes (1935:
1936) asked experienced examiners to mark a number of examination scripts. Examiners disagreed over the marks awarded to
scripts and even about the rank order of these scripts. The
following year the same examiners were asked to mark the same
scripts again and not only were disagreements discovered but
the examiners altered their grades considerably from those of
the previous year. Hence, the subjectivity of marking is so
great that it is not possible for the same piece of written work
to receive the same grade (even merely, fail, pass and credit)
on different occasions. It would, therefore, be possible to pass
on one day and fail on another with the same paper being
marked by the same assessor. Hence the replicability of the
results appears to be suspect, even in grading unchanged
written work. It is hardly surprising, therefore, that there has
been a movement towards more objective forms of testing.

Examinations Should Be Fair

It may be seen from the whole of this discussion that underlying
much of the argument is the idea that candidates in any examination system should be treated fairly. In this instance, fairness
may relate to freedom from discrimination, justice, impartiality,
honesty, etc. Most examinations employ procedures that ensure
freedom from discrimination and impartiality. Hence, in these
instances all candidates have an equal chance of demonstrating
the level of their competency to the examiners. In order to
ensure justice and honesty, procedures should be laid down and
followed carefully, yet the subjectivity of the actual assessment
raises questions about the extent to which it can be claimed that
examinations are fair and just. If one candidate is failed by
internal and external examiners on one day who would have
passed on another, can it be claimed that the system is totally
fair and just?

It may be claimed that the root of the problem of examinations
revolves around this issue of fairness and justice. Procedures
may be specified and precautions taken to guarantee that no
individual is discriminated against and that every candidate has

an equal chance to demonstrate his worth. Yet because standards
are subjective, it is possible that some candidates fail examinations whom other examiners would have passed, and vice versa.
Hence, the discrimination of those who are given the power and
responsibility to examine remains a subjective matter. Thus
attempts have been made to introduce more sophisticated stan-
dardising techniques and more objective examination questions.
These may overcome some of the problems associated with assessment, especially in practical and oral situations.

It may, therefore, be asked why examinations should be fair
to the candidates. After all, if the professions accepted sufficient
recruits of adequate standard, should they be concerned about
the unfortunate ones who are not given an opportunity to practice? In the first instance, adequate and best are not synonymous, and professions should seek the best for their clients, so
that they should always seek those best equipped to enter
practice. At the same time, it is contrary to the principles of
natural justice, and to the meaning of human life, not to institute
fair examination systems. If education is a humanistic process
then the systems of examining that are introduced should reflect
the high ideal of the process itself.

CURRICULUM EVALUATION

It is usually agreed that there are four basic elements in the
curriculum: aims and objectives, content, method and evaluation.
The last of these forms the basis for this brief discussion. Like
the other terms employed in this chapter, evaluation means
placing a value upon, or ascertaining the worth of the relevant
phenomenon, object of process. In this case, it refers to placing
a value upon the curriculum process, a process which may be
analysed in the context of the other three elements. However,
it may initially be asked who is the evaluator of the curriculum?
Frequently, tutors ask students to evaluate the course that they
have studied. Often tutors undertake their own review of the
course and, occasionally, researchers are asked to conduct a
more formal evaluation of a curriculum (see, for instance, Jarvis
and Gibson 1980). Certainly employers and sponsors also evaluate
courses. However, curriculum evaluators have been faced with
similar difficulties to those discussed earlier, that the values that
they place upon the process are their own, so that it may be
more important to provide information rather than actually to
evaluate the process. Hamilton (1976: 39) summarises some
approaches that have been introduced in order to do this and
which also seek to avoid the problems of subjectivity of values.

> Responsive evaluation responds to the wide range of questions
> asked about an innovation and is not trapped inside the
> intentions of the programme builders. Holistic evaluation seeks
> to portray an education programme in its entirety. Illuminative

evaluation (and this is the term that occurs most frequently) seeks to open out an educational situation to intelligent criticisms and appraisal.

While these forms of evaluation attempt to report upon the process and to highlight various aspects of it, they do not overcome the obstacles raised by placing a value upon an educational process. Students still evaluate the process, academic staff still do the same and sponsors and validators also seek to discover the worth of what is provided. In professional education, it is clear that both the process and the product of the process are important in the evaluation.

If the main concern in curriculum evaluation is the product of professional education, a form of utilitarianism would operate. This position was discussed briefly earlier and the major point to be spotlighted was that the value of the educational process is judged by the non-educational end-product, i.e. the practice of the professional. Hence it may be argued that since the practitioner is judged as competent, it matters not how he acquired his knowledge, skill and attitudes. He might have been indoctrinated, instructed or taught; he might have been given no other opportunity to explore the area of his subject competency nor to develop a critical awareness; he might have hated every moment of his training. Hence, if a teleological form of evaluation is adopted, then the means by which he acquired his expertise may be regarded as insignificant compared to the end-product. Clearly then, this is an approach to evaluation that educationalists should eschew.

Such an approach may, however, be that adopted by sponsors who might be more concerned with the cost-effectiveness of the professional education. If the product of the process is acceptable, then it should be achieved in the least time and at the lowest cost. Economic rationality must, obviously, play some part in the evaluation of the curriculum process but to ascribe the worth to the product in terms of economics and practice, but with no reference to the process appears to be a dangerous undertaking and one which educators in the profession should not accept. Nevertheless, it is necessary to recognise that the employer or sponsor does require some return on his investment - a level of competency in those who enter employment - and the frequent accusation that new recruits to a profession need a great deal of additional training may suggest that some employers do not consider that they always get a return on their money. Such accusations should be listened to by educators in the profession, so that if the complaint is justified, the curriculum content can be adjusted and made more relevant to the demands.

By contrast, the process is often evaluated by both academic staff and students. In many courses students are presented with questionnaires designed by the staff in order to help them revise the curriculum while in others staff and students hold review sessions together. The criteria for evaluating the process in this way also require investigation. There is a danger that occasionally the hedonistic principle may predominate when students evaluate the methods by which the content was presented to them, e.g. students who are used to formal lectures might not like group discussion, so that they are more critical of discussion sessions. While enjoyment is an important element in learning, it may not be the only criterion of judgement in relation to teaching and learning situations. Occasionally, for instance, provocations or traumatic experiences may result in more effective learning - not that either approach is necessarily beneficial to all or many students, but these might be evaluated by the students as being good.

It might be objected at this point that the main element of the curriculum is not the process but the content, so that it is important that curriculum evaluation should also concentrate upon the content learned as well as the teaching and learning methods employed. Clearly there is some foundation in this accusation, but as Houle (1980: 2254) points out:

> Widespread dissatisfaction with a purely content-centred approach to continuing professional education arose in the 1960's because of the all too apparent fact that it was not working satisfactorily. Bodies of knowledge were, for the most part, being adequately transmitted to practitioners by the medium of printed and oral presentations, but the transmission did not seem to be having the effect desired. Either working professionals were not absorbing the information available to them or they were not putting what they know into practice.

Educationalists, therefore, have been as much concerned with the process model as with the content model. Nevertheless, process without any content is of no more value than is content without process; hence, it is important to evaluate the actual content of the curriculum. In the fourth chapter some of the basic criteria by which curriculum content might be selected were outlined and these may form an important basis for evaluating the content included in the teaching and learning process.

Occasionally in curriculum evaluations undertaken by students, academic teachers are appraised and commented upon either in written questionnaires or orally in a review session. On the surface this appears to be a situation that should be avoided partly because it seems insensitive and also because it appears unprofessional. But it might be argued that one of the reasons why a number of the professions have been criticised in recent years, by such writers as Illich et al. (1977), is precisely because they have been insensitive to the criticisms of their clients. Hence, it may be argued that all professionals should be receptive to criticisms made about them by their clients, consider the extent of the criticism's validity and adapt their practice accordingly. This is even more important in education since it is a humanistic process where one of its most frequently occurring elements is the human interaction between teacher and learner. Because education involves human interaction, all personal criticism, whether it is the teacher criticising the learner or the learner criticising the teacher, should be undertaken sensitively, recognising once again that the criteria for evaluation are personal and subjective and that the human being receiving the criticism is both unique and invaluable. Yet the teacher might learn from the appraisal by his students and, thereafter, render even better service to them.

Finally, the aims and objectives require evaluation. In the third chapter it was argued that aims are broadly philosophical and three major aims were discussed. If these aims are accepted as a basis for professional education, any course may be evaluated holistically to see the extent to which they are achieved. However, little has been written in this study about objectives because specific curriculum issues have not been focused upon. Nevertheless, a teacher may seek to evaluate the extent to which say a single session, a module or short course, has achieved his objectives. If an objectives approach to teaching is employed, it is also necessary for the educator to ensure that his own teaching and learning objectives are valid in relation to the aims of the course overall.

Thus it may be seen that the aims and criteria may provide the basis of evaluation as to the extent to which objectives and content are valid. By contrast, other evaluations made of curricula are based upon subjective values, the criteria of which are themselves debatable.

CONCLUSION

Assessment, examination and evaluation all involve assessing the standards of practice of the educational assignments, the practitioner and the process. Few of those standards have objective measures of correctness, such as assessing the correctness of the application of a mathematical formula to a practical engineering problem. Some of the evaluations have criteria by which they may be assessed, such as the content of the curriculum. By contrast, many are based upon a considerable degree of subjectivity even though in some instances they are presented with a degree of spurious objectivity that can be misleading. Education, however, remains a humanistic process of learning, in which it is impossible to escape from having to define what is good practice or correct knowledge. Creating the ability to distinguish between good and bad practice and valid and invalid knowledge, is at the heart of the educational process itself and one of the aims of professional education. Hence, there is a sense in which the process of becoming educated is a process of acquiring the ability to evaluate and to appraise.

8   TEACHERS AND TEACHING IN THE EDUCATION

OF PROFESSIONALS

One consequence of the process of professionalisation has been
that the majority of professions in the United Kingdom have
placed much of their education and training in institutions of
further and higher education, and many teachers in the professions are now employed by universities or by local education
authorities in polytechnics and colleges of further education. In
some instances an agreement has been reached between the profession and the educational institution, so that the teacher is
actually employed by the profession but seconded to the educational institution. Yet in other instances, notably medicine,
the teacher is also a practitioner and teaching hospitals have,
consequently, acquired additional prestige because of the
prominent specialists who practise there but who also teach in
the local university. This is an ideal aspired to by other professions, such as accountancy (see Carlsberg 1976: 18-19).
However, the important point is that, with these notable excep-
tions, the educators of professionals are actually employed as
teachers of their discipline rather than practitioners of it. It is
this category upon which the ensuing discussion is focused;
the chapter itself having two main sections - teachers in the
professions and teaching in the professions.

TEACHERS IN THE PROFESSIONS

Considerable emphasis has been placed upon the twin elements
of theory and practice in this study. This distinction was also
quite explicit in the introduction to this chapter where it was
noted that most teachers in the professions are not employed as
practitioners as well. Perhaps medicine is the most obvious case
of the theoretician also being a practitioner, and the picture of
the consultant teaching his students at the patient's bedside is
one with which nearly everybody is familiar. However, a less
familiar picture is of the clinical nurse tutor teaching the
student nurses in the ward and yet some professions, such as
nursing, actually employ two grades of teacher - the one to
teach the theory and the other to teach the application of theory
to practice in the clinical situation: both will be discussed in
this section.

The Teacher of Theoretical Knowledge

The teacher in the professions is expected to be a master of the
discipline, or a sub-discipline, upon which professional practice
is based. Hence, the recruits to the profession are expected to
learn their theory from the specialist during their professional
basic education. Yet the theoretician may practise but rarely,
so that his knowledge might become rarified and distant from
the demands of practice. He may be interested in solving problems that are but of little concern to the practitioner and hence
the oft-quoted accusation that many university teachers occupy
ivory towers. Yet Carlsberg (1976: 19) notes how universities
have had a profound effect upon accountancy which he describes
as 'a revolution in accounting comparable to the industrial revolution in technology'. Clearly the university teacher is expected
to grapple with the profound problems of the discipline and
research is one of his major occupations. Yet he is a teacher!
It was pointed out in the previous chapter that few teachers in
higher education are expected to be trained in the skills of
teaching prior to employment as a teacher. Indeed, it is
interesting to note that nursing actually licenses its practitioners
to teach. However, as a teacher, the educator of professionals
has a daunting task of being both a master of his discipline and
an expert in the art of teaching it. Small wonder that the latter
has been regarded by some as being of lesser significance.
   Underlying this concern that the teacher should be the master
of his subject has been the assumption that the teacher is
intrinsically a part of the education process. Yet it has been
argued here that the learner is intrinsic to learning, whereas
the teacher is ancilliary to it - he is not so important to the
process and may be a facilitator of learning as much as an
exponent of knowledge. Hirst and Peters (1970: 77) touch upon
this point and claim that 'much serious miseducation can result
if too much attention is paid to it'. This claim suggests that
learning must occur only along the direction that the older
generation desire and, as such, raises questions about the extent
to which education, as they see it, may be regarded as indoctrination. Naturally, they are discussing children's education
rather than adult learning but, nevertheless, they do imply that
education may be a closed-end process.
   Yet the art of teaching is still something that the teacher
needs to acquire. The teacher of recruits to the profession still
needs to understand learning theory, the art of communication,
the art of planning lessons and other relevant topics. Yet it is
often claimed that the untrained teacher will learn from his
experience. This is true: but his students become his guinea
pigs, so that it must be asked if it is moral to expose learners
to an untrained teacher who may fail to communicate knowledge
or facilitate learning as effectively as he might have done had
he been trained? Thus it is suggested that failure to employ
trained or qualified teachers may be unethical. Clearly it could

be argued that some people are born communicators and can perform the teaching role without preparation and, while there may
be substance in the argument for the few, it does not necessarily
hold good for the many. Only by education can most teachers be
liberated from traditional methods and ideas and serve their
learners better by employing techniques which facilitate their
learning.

The Teachers of Practical Knowledge

In architecture the students are under supervision of their
schools during their two years practical experience; in civil
engineering 'the work of a trainer must be personally supervised
by a practising member of the Institute of Civil Engineers, and
is divided between site and office training' (Morton 1976: 69);
the newly fledged barrister has to find his own pupilage and
must be apprenticed to an experienced barrister for twelve
months; in social work the students are supervised by field work
teachers. Field work teachers are also to be found in health visiting, practical work teachers in district nursing and clinical
teachers in general nursing. In nearly every instance, the
practical teacher is also a practising professional. Thus it may
be seen that teachers of practical knowledge vary between professions: in some the teacher is a recognised specialist and
undergoes training whereas in others the students' training is
supervised by a professional practitioner.

Frequently it appears to be assumed that any practising professional can transmit the skills of his profession to one who has
learned some, or much, of the theoretical foundation. Clearly
this assumption is perfectly valid because skills learning has
occurred. Yet has it occurred as effectively as it might have
done had there been practising professionals trained as practical
teachers to undertake the task? There does not appear to be
sufficient evidence to argue that it is essential for the effective-
ness of the acquisition of skills that professions should train
some practitioners to assume a part-time teaching role. Nevertheless, it does appear logical that if there are skills to be
learned and techniques exist to help students learn the skills,
that those undertaking the teaching task should at least be
familiar with the techniques appropriate to it.

Since practical skills are less prestigious than theoretical
knowledge it is hardly surprising that few of the professions
have actually instituted a specific practical work teacher function
and that few train those who undertake it. Even those professions who have practical work teachers regard them as
accountable to the teacher of theoretical knowledge. This raises
questions of value which will be analysed in the final chapter.

The medical model of the practitioner who is also a theoretician
and a teacher of practical skills is one to which other professions
aspire and Carlsberg (1976: 19) advocates it for accountancy.
Yet not all medical practical work training is actually conducted

by the consultant on his rounds. Beswick (1976: 57-8) records
how medical students spend their second clinical year outside
of teaching hospitals and how they are then dispensed to work
with 'doctors and others who are actually doing the real job';
he does not record whether they are all trained to undertake the
work of practical teaching, although there are medical practices
that are designated trainee general practitioner practices.

Educating and Training Teachers in the Professions

Much of the above discussion has concentrated upon the fact
that training to teach in the professions has been less rigorous,
and indeed considered less necessary than training in professional competence. This reflects two distinct but related
questions: the first relates to the fact that there are effective
communicators of knowledge and skills whose ability appears to
come without training in the theory and practice of teaching, so
why is such education necessary?; the second asks whether there
is a discipline of education anyway? Each of these two questions
will be discussed briefly.

The sceptic who claims that there is no need for teacher training in the professions must be taken seriously because, for so
long, the practice of not training teachers has been accepted
and it appears to have done the profession no harm. Yet it needs
be asked whether evidence exists to justify the retention of the
status quo. Certainly there is considerable research evidence in
the education of adults to suggest that learning can be made more
effective if skilled teaching techniques are employed, even
though educators of adults consider that this is a much neglected
field of study (Knowles 1978). If research in the education of
adults suggests that the learning can be more effective if techniques other than the traditional teaching approaches are
employed, then it appears logical that those whose task it is to
teach adults should be aware of the research evidence and that
they should gain experience in practising those other approaches.
It is claimed here, therefore, that the sceptic's position may
actually be illogical because of its failure to recognise and consider the research that has been undertaken in learning among
adults.

Another factor preventing the professions from introducing
schemes for training the trainers may be that the resources are
not readily available at present in the United Kingdom. Such an
argument must be conceded since very few universities and polytechnics have actually introduced courses of training for educators in the professions, although this deficiency is being
rectified at the time of writing. Yet there is but a gradual
acceptance of the need for teachers of practical and theoretical
knowledge in the professions to undertake educational studies to
fit them for their role. This appears illogical, considering the
professions' own emphases on the need for training prior to
entry into their ranks.

But it could be argued that professions are based upon a discipline of knowledge as well as one of skill, whereas education is merely a matter of technique plus a number of different academic perspectives upon a process. This resurrects an argument that is at least a century old since Scheffler (1973: 82) records how the first annual convention of American normal-school principals in 1859 passed a resolution proclaiming that 'education is a science'. Resolutions, or not, education is not yet universally accepted as an academic discipline but, despite this rather sterile discussion, educationalists have continued to debate whether the art and the science of teaching children (pedagogy) is distinct from the art and science of helping adults learn (andragogy). Malcolm Knowles (1978: 1980), is perhaps the most well known exponent of andragogy but even he (1980: 43) now claims that andragogy and pedagogy 'are probably most useful when seen not as dichotomous but rather as two ends of a spectrum'. However, the fact remains that the debate about andragogy, pedagogy and even humanagogy, has been based upon empirical research, therefore, it appears that research is in the process of creating a body of knowledge derived from several disciplines which might be called education knowledge. Is this knowledge necessary in order to be a teacher of adults? In response, it appears desirable and logical that, if knowledge exists that may enable a teacher in the professions to perform his role more effectively, he should learn this and also learn the skills of its application.

However, this produces a situation in which an individual is expected to be knowledgeable about two academic disciplines and skilled in their practice, even though he may not be expected to practise in his initial profession. Failure, however, to practise in that profession may be detrimental to his teaching of it because the academic, theoretical teacher may be concerned with theoretical issues that are of less concern or relevance to the students in their professional basic education than they are to the teacher and his peers. Yet too much concern with the practice might hinder the growth of theoretical and empirical research which constitutes a part of the work of the teacher in many of the professions. This, then, raises some of the issues that will be examined in the ensuing part of this chapter.

TEACHING IN THE PROFESSIONS

The teacher in the professions is confronted with a number of problems, all of which are relevant to teachers in higher education generally. Some of them will be explored briefly here in relation to professional education, under the following four sub-headings: the professionalism of the teacher of professionals; the authority of the teacher of professionals; the teacher of professionals and academic freedom; responsibility and accountability in professional education.

The Professionalism of the Teacher of Professionals

Implicit in the discussion earlier was the idea that teaching may
be a separate profession having its own theoretical knowledge,
skills and demanding its own professional ideology. Yet a person
who is employed by an educational institution to teach the
theoretical and practical knowledge of another profession is also
usually a member of that profession. Hence he is, by virtue of
his occupation of teacher, a member of two professions, and
expected to have expertise in both. It is hardly surprising that
universities have traditionally been more concerned about the
academic competency of the member of staff in their professional
discipline than in education. Indeed, the teacher is expected to
be a researcher, generating new knowledge and ideas in his
professional discipline and also publishing this for his professional colleagues to evaluate. Thereafter, he is expected to
be a teacher of that professional discipline to students. It
follows, therefore, that the teacher who conducts research,
generates new knowledge and publishes it widely abroad for
his colleagues may be viewed as an important member of the
profession. If he also practises that professional discipline, he
may be able to explore his own theories in practice and, consequently, ensure that his research and theory are relevant to
the actual working situation of many of his colleagues.

It follows quite logically from this that the teacher, who is
also trying to be the researcher, the writer and the practitioner
in his original discipline will find it quite difficult to be the
master and skilled practitioner of another discipline, namely,
education. This it seems is a constant dilemma for the teacher
in the professions - wherein is he to put his energies?

Clearly the significance of research to professions means that
those who have demonstrated their theoretical knowledge in the
profession should be involved with the generation of new knowledge. Hence it is logical to place responsibility for research in
institutions of higher education. However, research, especially
if it is of an empirical nature, does not demand the full-time
energies of the experienced professional, so that research assist-
ants undertake much of the more mundane research tasks. This
frees the teacher to perform other tasks, such as keeping
abreast with publications in his field, writing, practising his
profession and teaching. However, in much of this, the teacher
is actually practising his initial profession and is involved,
therefore, in a content approach to the curriculum rather than
a process one.

A similar argument may obtain in the case of practical skills
teachers who spend the majority of the time in professional
practice. When they have a student placed with them, they are
still expected to continue with their professional practice, even
though they are also expected to undertake teaching. In this
instance, they are actually on-the-job and, consequently, the
student is an addition to the work load of the practitioner. The

Panel of Assessors has stipulated that a district nurse who undertakes the practical work teacher role should have her workload reduced by 25 per cent in order to allow her to fulfil her teaching role adequately. Yet the demands on the service are such that this may be an ideal rather than a practicality.

If a teacher in the professions were to put all of his energies into understanding the educational theory underlying his teaching practice, to planning his teaching sessions and to employing a variety of teaching techniques in order to stimulate learning, this might result in his being unable to conduct research or practise his original profession. Herein lies the dilemma: in which profession is the teacher of professionals and wherein lies his professionalism? Obviously there are preferences among those who are involved in teaching professionals and it might be argued that herein lies academic freedom; to concentrate upon research, professional practice or teaching. Yet this does raise problems! The teacher who concentrates upon research and professional practice may be a poor example of teaching, yet be employed to teach. He may have considerable knowledge, but not be able to assist students to learn it thoroughly; much professional skill, but not the ability to aid students to emulate him. In short, he may not be a professional teacher. Hence it is argued here that the professionalism of the teacher of professionals should be primarily directed towards being a teacher. This does not rule out research or practice, but makes the claim that the professionalism of the teacher should be primarily directed towards assisting the students to learn. In order for this to happen, it may mean that academic staff have to concentrate upon fewer areas of the professional discipline, so that they can spend more time on planning the teaching and learning. However, it is recognised that straddling two professions is both a difficult and demanding task for those who undertake it.

There are also those in professional practice who wish to or who are expected to undertake some teaching, although their first responsibility is towards being a professional practitioner. A similar case may be made for those whose first priority is research. Nevertheless, all who undertake some regular teaching responsibility in the professions should at least be expected to familiarise themselves with the art and science of teaching adults - hence the argument of this section is that, in the first instance, those employed to teach should direct their energies and skills first towards the students and their acquisition of knowledge and skill, for being a teacher demands a commitment to being a master of knowledge and skill to facilitate the students' learning.

The Authority of the Teacher of Professionals

If the above argument is taken to its logical extreme it would be possible to argue that the educators of professionals should concentrate upon education to the exclusion of their discipline.

It is this extreme position which, in relation to initial education of children, Bantock (1952: 202) attacks when he claims that the 'exhilaration of new found "methods" seems . . . to be contributing to the concealment of a very real restriction of scope and of a dangerous tendency to confuse means with ends, a state of affairs which is likely to lead . . . to a very definite decline in the quality of educational accomplishment . . .' However, this is not the position being advocated here. It was noted above that in order to be effective, teachers in professional education might have to restrict the scope of their work in the professional discipline to concentrate, for example, on fewer sub-disciplines. This in no way suggests that teachers should not retain their expertise in the content of their material, merely to reflect the reality of a situation in which, if they are to be professional teachers, they need to be aware of developments in two professional disciplines.

Indeed, it is advocated that in the education of adults the only authority the teacher possesses is that authority of being the master of the discipline he teaches and the expert in helping students to acquire that knowledge. Hence, in the first instance his authority stems from mastery of the subject which is being studied. Secondly, the teacher is regarded as being one who understands about learning and teaching, so that it is recognised that he is trying to provide the most adequate conditions in which learning may occur. Herein lies his authority: it is the authority of the professional and it is recognised by those who study with him. This is the authority of the discipline rather than the authority to discipline others.

Clearly the educator of professionals does not have the same type of problems with his learners as does the school teacher with children. Adults who come to learn have at least different motivations, more advanced social skills and a different perspective upon learning. There is little need to discuss authority to discipline in the context of classroom behaviour in professional education: in those rare instances where problems occur, they are matters of social interaction and interpersonal skills, rather than authority. Nevertheless, some professions, such as nursing, regard their teachers as officers of management. Directors of nurse education and senior tutors may be involved in professional grievance procedures and designated as being the person to whom the student is accountable. In these instances the educator is occupying a management role and then the exercise of authority is by virtue of the position occupied in the bureaucratic hierarchy rather than as a result of professional expertise. Such a distinction must be clearly made since these are two discrete types of authority and each will be briefly explored.

Professional authority finds its legitimation in the recognition given to the practitioner by his peers, his clients and others that he is an expert and that his views are to be valued. It is similar to the charismatic leader, discussed by Max Weber (1947), where authority is legitimated by his followers. By contrast, bureaucratic authority is Weber's rational-legal authority, legitimated by the rules and regulations of the employing organisation and making no reference to the teacher, his peers or his learners; in short, it is the authority of office.

Obviously, the authority of the educator in the professions is mostly of a professional type but there are instances, e.g. selection interviewing, where his authority stems from the rational-legal procedures, by which the organisation of the profession vests authority in the academic to select or reject certain applicants to the profession. Similarly, the nurse educator's position in the management hierarchy is a more explicit statement of the same form of authority. Since the role of an educator in the professions involves a variety of different facets, it must be recognised that the authority of these are not all legitimated by the same mechanism. Nevertheless, it may be clearly seen that the primary authority of the teacher is not to have power over people but to be recognised by them as having an expertise from which they, or other people, may benefit. It is this that contributes to 'the humanistic basis' of education and a reason for educators developing their own ideology of professionalism.

The Teacher of Professionals and Academic Freedom

Hall (1969: 82) regards the belief in autonomy of action as one of the attitudinal characteristics of professionals. By autonomy, he means:

> the feeling that the practitioner ought to be allowed to make his own decisions without external pressures from clients, from others who are not members of his profession, or from his employing organization.

In his empirical research among different professions in America, Hall did not actually record whether any of his respondents were teachers in their respective professions. Nevertheless, their autonomy is not absolute, as has been shown in previous chapters. A contractual relationship exists between the validating body and the teaching team when a course has the approval of a profession and/or from a validating body other than the profession. e.g. the Council for National Academic Awards, so that this constitutes a limiting factor to freedom.

Additionally, the teacher is the recipient of pressures from his students' learning needs, from the demands of professional practice, etc. and these limit his freedom. Of course, a teacher could ignore the learning needs of his students but this might result in many students boycotting teaching sessions and thus demonstrating that their needs are not being met.

Academic freedom does not, therefore, mean that the academic is free in an autonomous sense. He is not free: of the contract to teach the discipline; of the legitimate demands of colleagues and students; of the demands of his own professionalism. He is free: to search for the truth in his academic sphere; to express that truth without fear of reprisal; to engage his students in critical discussion of controversial topics within their profession. These things he can do because he is teaching adults who should be critically aware, able to understand and to sift the wheat from the chaff. Academic freedom is a noble concept that, in its essence, gives the academic and the student freedom to study without coercion or censorship and the academic institution freedom to decide what courses and research it will conduct. Once a profession has delegated responsibility to an educational institution it should not seek to censor nor correct it, although it is self-evident that if it is dissatisfied with its recruits' education, it has the right to remove its students or to request changes, even during the contracted period. But academic freedom means that the academic has the freedom to create a forum in which the truth is sought and in this sense the academic has a positive responsibility.

Responsibility and Accountability in Professional Education

It was clear from the previous section that freedom without responsibility may be a misuse of freedom, so that it is now necessary to explore the concept of responsibility. However, at the outset of this section it must be recognised that these two terms, responsibility and accountability, may at times be employed synonymously, so that it is important here to clarify how they are employed within this context. Accountability is to be responsible, or answerable, to someone for one's actions, so that the emphasis here is upon being under authority in some manner or other. By contrast, to be responsible means to have authority and to be able to take decisions without supervision. The manner in which these words are used here are similar to the distinction made earlier in this chapter between being an authority, i.e. a professional, and being in authority, i.e. a bureaucrat.

The teacher has responsibility, he may take decisions about what to teach, when to teach it and how to teach it based upon his own professional authority as being both competent in his discipline and in the appropriate methods of teaching and learning. His professional authority is acknowledged and legitimated by his colleagues, peers and students alike. For so long as that legitimation exists few would question the responsibility of the teacher. However, it is a responsibility for the teaching and the learning of students. It is a positive responsibility to provide students with the opportunity to search after the truth and to fulfil the aims of professional education. Even so, it is a responsibility that is not only derived from the professional expertise of the teacher but the relationship that the teacher has with the employing educational organisation. In this sense it is dependent upon the existential relationships between the professional and the organisation since the professional teacher is not an independent practitioner.

There is, therefore, a sense in which the teacher is accountable to his employing organisation for the educational process for which he is responsible. For as long as his professional authority is acknowledged, the accountability factor may not be very apparent but if ever the legitimation of professional authority is withdrawn by colleagues, peers or students, then the teacher may legitimately be called to account for his actions by the professional educational organisation. In this sense the professional teacher may be called to account by his professional organisation in the same manner as a professional practitioner may be called to account by his employer or his professional association, in the case of alleged malpractice.

CONCLUSION

This chapter has sought to examine some of the dilemmas surrounding the teacher and teaching in professional education. It has shown how the teacher is a member of two professions and that straddling both of these is a most demanding phenomenon. It has, nevertheless, argued strongly that the teacher should be as much a professional teacher as he is a professional practitioner in his original occupation, so that the demands of professionalism in teaching are also incumbent upon him. Clearly these demands are of a moral nature but because education is a humanistic process it can never avoid the ethical issues, some of which have been discussed in this chapter. Nevertheless, others that have arisen elsewhere in this study require examination and the final chapter turns its attention to some of these.

In the majority of instances the educational process involves
human interaction, between the learners and between teacher
and learner, so that the ethical issues involved in social inter-
course are of fundamental importance in any consideration of
education. Additionally, in professional practice social interaction occurs which involves moral issues, so that ethics should
be an intrinsic part of professional education. Yet often these
ethical issues remain undiscussed and, sometimes, even unasked
during the period of preparation for practice. Often the common
practice is assumed to be the answer to the unasked or undiscussed questions. Even so, further consideration of common
practice may raise issues and reveal that no clear-cut answers
can be provided legitimately to the moral questions involved in
both practice and the educational process. It is, therefore,
essential that some of these ethical issues are confronted in
professional education, even though it is acknowledged that no
more than a cursory introduction can be provided to some of
them here. Each of the issues selected is large enough for and
demands much further treatment than it receives, but the seven
areas to be examined have been selected because they have
occurred during the previous discussion. These are: professionalism as an ideology of commitment; the relationship between
theory, practice and attitudes in professional education;
educational processes, adulthood and humanity; education and
freedom; professional and personal development in the context
of basic and continuing professional education; a justification
for the education of professionals; the value of the human being.
Each of these issues forms a section of this chapter.

PROFESSIONALISM AS AN IDEOLOGY OF COMMITMENT

Professionalism, it has been argued, demands that the practitioner should be the master of professional knowledge and
skill, so that he can be of maximum service to his clients. Yet
embodied within this statement are two contradictory ideas -
mastery and service. It is hardly surprising that the implications
of mastery carry over into a relationship of professional dominance
with a client who may be ignorant in the area in which the practitioner excels. Such professional dominance is often ritualised
through employment of all the social-psychological techniques in
order to impress upon the client the high status of the prac-

titioner. Indeed, in contemporary society self-presentation has assumed a level of importance and significance which is at least questionable, although this will not be pursued here. Even so, it must be borne in mind that the image that the practitioner presents may be no more than a reflection of techniques employed which might hide a shallowness of commitment to the ideas of professionalism. Professionalism is not about display, it is about the reality of mastery of an area of knowledge and skill in order to be of service. In this sense, professionalism has little or nothing to do with self-presentation but it involves a commitment in order to respond to the concerns of others. This, then, is an altruistic ideal which needs considerable discussion before it is placed in the context of professional education and this will be undertaken by first, examining the concept of unprofessional practice; secondly, assessing the reasons why professionalism is good; finally, relating this discussion to professional education.

Unprofessional Practice

In everyday speech 'unprofessional practice' may be used to denote either that a practitioner has been disloyal to a colleague or to the profession itself in some manner, or that a practitioner has broken the code of ethics laid down by a professional association. Yet these ideas need some elaboration in order to investigate whether the usages actually relate to bad practice.

Loyalty to colleagues and to the professions may appear to be self-evidently 'good' on the surface, but is it always so? What if a practitioner is aware that a colleague will not render a person adequate professional service? What if he thinks that a decision taken by the professional association is not in the best interests of the general public? What if adherence to the ethics of the profession is going to result in the client receiving a reduced service? Loyalty may be regarded as a duty but it may result in the service rendered to the clients being less than the best. Herein lies the classical debate between deontological arguments (goodness is achieved by fulfilment of a duty) and teleological ones (goodness is achieved through maximising the benefits of the acts). Yet if professionalism involves service then in some way the end-product, or the intended end-product, should be of benefit to the client, rather than to fellow practitioners or to the profession in general. Nevertheless, it is recognised that professional associations, such as the British Medical Association, have often been accused of being powerful pressure groups on behalf of their members, rather than on behalf of their members' clients. The validity of this accusation is not a matter for discussion at this juncture although displaced goals are regarded by sociologists as one of the hallmarks of bureaucracy. Individual practitioners who also seek to exercise their practice for self-aggrandisement also corrupt the ideal of professionalism. Professionalism, it is maintained, involves a commitment that results in benefit to the client rather than necessarily to the practitioner. If the latter benefits as a result of his concern for his client, then there may be no corruption of the ideal.

What of the practitioner who spends so much time serving his clients that he has no time to keep abreast with latest developments in the field? This, it must be acknowledged, is a very possible danger and a dilemma that may confront many practitioners. No clear-cut answer exists. To serve the needs of many clients may be detrimental to the practitioner's attempt to keep abreast with recent developments – but failure to respond to another's need is also culpable, even if it results in the practitioner not devoting enough time to his own professional development. If, for example, as a result of the failure to keep abreast, a doctor does not know the treatment for a patient he may be considered blameworthy and unprofessional, yet this may have occurred out of his dedication to his patients. Hence it appears that the commitment of the professional ideology should be both to the mastery of the discipline and to the service of the clients, even though this may result in dilemmas that individual practitioners have to resolve for themselves. This is a real dilemma rather than an imaginary one, because it involves consideration of service rather than of selfishness.

Professionalism as Good

The professional seeks always to render to his client the best possible form of service – to do less than this would be, in the majority of instances, a denial of the professional's mastery of his discipline. More than this, it implies that the client is not worth the professional's effort and this is to deny the humanity of both the client and the practitioner. Yet to suggest that professionalism is an ideology devoted to the maximisation of the end-product is to imply that it is a utilitarian philosophy. In part this would be accepted, but not in its entirety, since the nature of both client and practitioner have to be considered. If, as a result of mastering an area of professional knowledge, the practitioner may achieve some personal development and as a result of service both the practitioner and the client may achieve the fulfilment of some of their human needs – then professionalism is good – not because of its utilitarian nature but judged on its value to the human being. Hence, it is argued here that the reason why professionalism is good is that its intended result may be beneficial to humanity, and the development of the mastery of the area of professional knowledge may be advantageous to the development of the practitioner: professionalism is good because of its overall value to humanity.

Thus it may be argued that in a time of rapidly expanding knowledge it is necessary for professional people to keep abreast with developments in their own field. Continued learning must be the outcome, even though this need not result in the provision of continuing education for everyone, since some may

actually undertake their own study programme. The provision
of continuing education may, therefore, be symbolic of the
expectation that professional practitioners will not otherwise
keep abreast, and that they do not have time to do so! Therefore, the provision of continuing education may reflect the
professional occupation's intention of encouraging all its members
to keep abreast with latest developments in order to ensure that
the client receives the best service.

Professionalism and Professional Education

Professionalism is an ideal of commitment for the sake of service.
It is, therefore, a moral issue which demands considerable study
and discussion since there are no simple solutions. It does not
involve indoctrination, rather it demands a considered examination of the values implicit in the concept and, as such, should
form a major focus in the professional education curriculum.

It is important that the high ideals of professionalism are not
lost from view and that it is recognised that this demands a moral
commitment to a way of life, perhaps best exemplified by the
Hippocratic Oath or the ordination vows of the priest. It is
hardly surprising that in this secular, rationalistic age this
perspective is less popular than other interpretations of the
concept. Yet it is a relevant one, especially in a society where
the knowledge and skills base of many professions are undergoing rapid change, so that the practitioner will be expected
to undertake additional learning and re-learning during his
career. The commitment may not be of a religious nature but,
nevertheless, professionalism remains an ideology of commitment
to mastery in order to serve. It is an ideology about 'good'
and 'bad' practice, about being committed to the former and
eschewing the latter and, as such, it should constitute a major
focus for professional education.

THE RELATIONSHIP BETWEEN THEORY, PRACTICE AND
ATTITUDES IN PROFESSIONAL EDUCATION

A major contention here is that education for the professions not
only involves educating recruits in the theory and practice of
their occupations but that, from the outset of their training, they
should learn about the commitment to professionalism i.e. they
should learn specific attitudes that might be regarded as relevant
to professional practice and unique to it. It has been noted that
the acquisition of these attitudes is important to the profession,
but it allows for the accusation of indoctrination to be levelled
at professional education. However, this accusation was rejected
earlier since any form of indoctrination, whether it is in aim,
content or method, is contrary to the humanistic base of education, and therefore should not be practised by educationalists.
Yet some professions have actually specified attitudes that relate

to certain aspects of knowledge and skill and which practitioners should acquire. In these instances, it is much more likely that the charge of indoctrination might have more substance, since the profession seems to be attempting to stereotype the practitioner and to fit him into a mould. This is quite contrary to the concept of education which was propounded earlier since it allows little or no opportunity for the individual to develop his own perspectives upon specific elements of professional practice. If the content of the professional ideology is specified by the profession then indoctrination may occur. But students should be encouraged to study 'professionalism' during their education or training, so that they may be given opportunity to work out for themselves what it actually means to them to be a professional, committed to attempting to master the skills and knowledge necessary to practise the occupation and to serve clients. Hence, the education of professionals is also about helping the individual prepare himself for practice as much as it is about giving him the necessary knowledge and skill to embark upon his professional career. Preparation of the person may be as important as is the provision of the tools to practise. Indeed, if the person has the tools but not the commitment he may be able to serve the client better initially than the person who has the motivation but neither the knowledge nor the skill. But he may also fail to serve some to the full who need him because of his lack of commitment. Often, it is claimed, the preparation of the person occurs through professional socialisation, as part of the hidden curriculum in the education and training of the professional. Professional socialisation certainly does occur during basic education, but whether it produces ideological commitment to service is by no means proven. Indeed, the process is neither overt nor always carefully planned, but it seems logical to emphasise the preparation of the person for his role as much as it is to provide him with the knowledge and skill necessary to undertake the demands of his professional practice.

Some professions, such as school teaching and social work, place considerable emphasis on the practical skills of the occupation, whereas others place far greater emphasis on the knowledge base of practice. As was argued earlier, this knowledge base needs to be broadened in order to incorporate other forms of knowledge relevant to professional practice. Nevertheless, it was also pointed out that knowledge is high status, whereas skills are regarded as low status. Michael Young (1971: 38), referring to school knowledge, suggests that the dominant characteristics of high-status knowledge are that it is: abstract, literate, individualistic and unrelated to non-school knowledge. Thus, he is claiming that the more theoretical and unrelated to the world of everyday, the greater the status of the knowledge. Clearly he is correct, in as far as theory is ascribed greater esteem than practice. This is also apparent in the way that the term 'education' has become a slogan vested with status whereas the word 'training' relates to skills and has less esteem. This

emphasis is clearly apparent in most areas of professional education where the theory is seen to be more important than the
practice. Recently, for instance, district nursing introduced a
new curriculum for the education and training of its recruits.
Prior to the introduction of this curriculum, 62.5 per cent of
the time was devoted to practice but in the new curriculum only
33.3 per cent of the time is given to this. The significance of
this change is even greater when it is realised that prior to
this new curriculum, most district nurses were trained on an
in-service basis, so that they actually had practical experience
prior to commencing their course of training but, concurrently
with the introduction of the new course, district nursing introduced mandatory training as a criterion to entering the service,
so that in future all new recruits will be trained before they
enter practice.

Why should theory be of higher status than practical skills?
Obviously, this has a long history for it was only the elite,
leisure classes in bygone generations who had the time to read
the classics and to practise the arts, and it may be that the
status of cognitive knowledge may be traced to its association
with the upper classes. As Young (1971: 38) suggests, an
'educational system based on a model of bookish learning for
medieval priests which was extended first to lawyers and doctors
and increasingly has come to dominate all education of older age
groups in industrial societies'. This perspective has also been
reinforced by the traditional approach to teaching, in which the
teacher provides the theory in general, abstract terms which
the students then learn to apply to the specific concrete situation. Deduction from the general to the particular has traditionally been an element of the philosophy of teaching. Induction
from a set of specific premises or experiences to the general
has been something of a rarity in teaching apart from in empirical
scientific research. Thus the theoretical and abstract have the
higher status. But is this justified in the modern industrial
world? One of the characteristics of contemporary society is its
fragmentation, so that there has grown up an interdependence
between its parts. Emile Durkheim (1933) characterised modern
society's structure as being 'organic' i.e. complex, interdepen-
dent and like an organism. The concept of interdependence is
quite significant in modern society, so that one element of
society cannot function efficiently without another. To be whole,
society needs all of its separate entities, including people whose
work is devoted primarily to the practical skills and those whose
work concentrates upon the theoretical aspects.

Thus far the argument from interdependence rests solely on a
sociological premise. However, a similar argument may be cited
from the human being. The theoretician, who is most impractical,
appears as incomplete in some ways as the practitioner who is
unable to pursue his thoughts to great depths. Indeed, the
professional who has the knowledge but not the skills may be of no
more value to his client than the one who has the skills rather

than the knowledge. Clearly then both the knowledge and the skills are valuable in the practice of the profession: to elevate the one at the expense of the other is to do both a disservice. Yet a number of professions, including teaching in higher education, still place little emphasis on the practical skills of the occupation!

It is maintained then that theory and practice are equally important in the practice of a professional occupation and the practical should be considered as equally worthwhile as the theoretical, so that professional education needs to incorporate both, in relevant proportions, within the curriculum.

EDUCATIONAL PROCESSES, ADULTHOOD AND HUMANITY

A traditional image of education, especially in some institutions of higher education, is of the lecturer entering the lecture theatre, expounding his knowledge to the students who listen or take notes so that they can learn and regurgitate these in the necessary examination. Having given his lecture, the teacher leaves the room. He has instructed the students and he regards his teaching role as having been fulfilled. Thereafter, it is the responsibility of the students to learn. They can seek an appointment, if necessary, in order to see him and discuss queries that they might have. Little, or no, human interaction occurs between lecturer and students in the lecture; their roles are distinct and separate. It has been an impersonal transmission of knowledge, but the nature of the process denies something of the humanity of the learners who have been placed in the position of being passive recipients of the expert's exposition. Yet it might be claimed that since the teacher's authority rests on his expertise the students should listen respectfully to his position. Undeniably the teacher should be respected for his knowledge but even more so for his humanity. But in the position described here the learners' own knowledge and experience have not been respected and little, or no, human interaction has occurred between them and the lecturer, so that the humanistic basis of education is called into question. Is there then no place for the traditional lecture in the education of adults? This is a contentious point but if the teaching method prohibits the manifestation of, or fails to respect, the humanity of the learners it becomes a questionable educational exercise.

The traditional approach to education assumes what Freire (1972: 46) calls the banking concept of education in which, 'knowledge is a gift bestowed by those who consider themselves knowledgeable upon those whom they consider to know nothing'. While Freire may be overstating his case here, it illustrates a conception of man that requires consideration: man as an empty container needing filling or a computer waiting to receive and store knowledge. It is at this point that the humanity of the learners needs to be considered in the educational process.

The position outlined here is not far from the conception of man underlying McGregor's theory X, which has been applied to education (Davies 1971: 158-60). This suggests that the teacher adopts the teaching style that he does because he assumes the human being has:

(a) an inherent dislike of studying so that he will avoid it if he can;
(b) to be coerced, controlled, directed, threatened so that he does learn;
(c) to be directed in what and how he learns because he wishes to avoid responsibility to do so for himself.

Often these assumptions are implicit in much initial education. Consider how a naughty boy is kept in school and given additional mathematics to do while the good boy is allowed out early. Going to school and learning are punishments, and that is what the child learns. In both of these illustrations a residue of the Christian doctrine of fallen man is to be discovered. The worst is expected of the human being rather than the best, because that is in the nature of the beast.

Yet man is not only a receptacle in which knowledge is stored, nor is he necessarily lazy or unmotivated to learn, although this is not to deny that he may actually appear to be some of these things by the time he enters professional education because he has become conditioned to being treated in this way. But to do this is to dehumanise him and in so doing it is contrary to the basis of education itself as formulated in the definition used here. Education is a humanistic process in which the participants should be able to fulfil their own human potential, develop their selves and learn to be. Hence Knowles (1978) argued that, in contrast to pedagogy, andragogy respected the maturity of the adult learner who brought with him a self-concept of essential self-direction, a reservoir of experience, a readiness to learn and a motivation to learn from a problem-centred starting point. Knowles initially considered andragogy to be distinct from pedagogy but in his latest publications (1980) he recognises that the assumptions of andragogy may be relevant to the education of children as well. Knudson (1980) argued that since education is about human beings in teaching and learning situations both the terms pedagogy and andragogy should be replaced by the ugly concept of 'humanagogy'. While his term has not received any currency, it must be recognised that the human being is at the heart of the educational process. Thus it is maintained here that the moral connotations of the process are such that the humanity of all the participants must be respected and developed in education. Failure to do this falls short of the humanistic basis of education itself.

EDUCATION AND FREEDOM

Freedom is a concept traditionally associated with education and in the previous chapter the concept of academic freedom was discussed in some detail. Yet there are a number of other issues that are quite crucial to the understanding of the relationship between education and freedom that are discussed here. But before this is done, it is necessary to recognise that freedom takes a number of different forms and each relates to both education in general and to professional education in particular. It would be difficult to claim that anyone is totally free, because the individual is 'what he is' as a result of his previous knowledge and experience. For instance, it would be most difficult to claim that a person brought up in a strict puritan household who had acquired a very rigid code of moral behaviour is really free to break that code, if he were to be given the opportunity to do so. Yet the mere fact that the opportunity may arise indicates that it is possible to conceive of freedom in terms of the external constraints that an individual experiences. However, a person may feel pressurised by external social constraints yet still know that legally he is free to follow his own pursuits. Therefore, it may be seen that freedom may be conceived as being free from either internal, external or legal constraints. A combination of these forms of freedom may occur in any given situation, but for purposes of clarity the following discussion is based upon these three types of freedom.

Freedom from Internal Constraint

As a result of primary socialisation, biological constitution and personality characteristics everyone has certain constraints to his behaviour and yet the educational process can free the individual from many of these pressures. Perhaps the most well known exponent of this is Paulo Freire (1972), who sought to create an adult literacy learning environment in which Brazilian peasants could become conscious of the reality of their situation and of the falsity of their own perceptions of social reality. Yet had the peasants been taught only to read and write, it is doubtful that Freire would have been regarded as a threat by the political elite. Education freed them from the internal constraints imposed upon them as a result of their socialisation into a perception of a dominant cultural reality. In precisely the same manner education may free other individuals from internal constraints and make them free to work for change. If professional education is truly an educational process then it will free recruits from their initial perceptions and constraints.

Freedom from External Constraints

If the aim of education is to produce individuals who are critically aware then the educated person should be free to assess the external constraints that act upon him and to respond to them accordingly. This may mean that educated persons are individuals who are not necessarily conformists. Hence, two elements emerge here. Initially, undergoing an educational process has an individuating effect, as a result of which the person is freed to be himself; he is freed to be different, or to conform, because he can make a choice based upon his mastery of knowledge and skill. Therefore, professionals should not necessarily conform to the expectation of others. The second point is that critical awareness frees the professional to resist external pressures of which he may disapprove. This is very important in professional practice, especially if the professional is employed in a bureaucratic organisation where standardised procedures, etc. are a permanent feature of the organisational structure. It is a small wonder that Miller (1967), among other researchers, discovered that engineers and industrial scientists suffered alienation from work as a result of being a professional and working in a bureaucratic environment.

Education and Legal Constraints

From the above discussion, it is clear that the critically aware, educated professional will be individuated and may not necessarily be a conformist. Yet freedom is not antinomianism, so that to be free is not to disregard laws, rules or regulations. Yet conforming to rules and regulations is not the sole criterion of goodness, so that the professional may seek other means of doing what he considers to be right which might result in his being an innovator and, perhaps, regarded as a radical.

Education not only frees the individual to evaluate the internal and external constraints upon him, a rather negative approach to freedom, it also frees him to be positive. It frees him to develop ways by which he can best serve his clients, develop new approaches to his practice and allows him the opportunity to discover and develop himself.

PERSONAL AND PROFESSIONAL DEVELOPMENT IN THE CONTEXT OF BASIC AND CONTINUING PROFESSIONAL EDUCATION

Dewey wrote:

> Since life means growth, a living creature lives as truly and positively at one stage as at another, with the same instinctive fullness and the same absolute claims. Hence education means the enterprise of supplying the conditions which insure growth, or adequacy of life, irrespective of age. (1961: 51)

While Dewey's categorical 'the enterprise' is disputed here since individuals grow and develop through means other than edu-

cation, it is certainly true that education may assist growth:
for it will be recalled that mention was made above of how education
helps the individual to develop a sense of independence
and the ability to withstand any social pressures exerted upon
him to conform. Yet to grow and to develop are difficult phrases
to understand. Individuals grow, in the sense of ageing, until
they die. Not all, however, age gracefully. Some may never
grow into 'rounded' human beings to whom others turn for
advice, guidance and comfort. Not all who are educated develop
the type of personality which others trust or from whom they
would seek advice. The direction of growth, therefore, remains
undefined. Ideally, it might be claimed that the graceful, loving,
trusting and trustworthy person is the type of person into
which all might like to grow. Education may help achieve ends
such as these, but it is by no means certain that the process of
education, ipso facto, changes the personality of the one being
educated. Claims for this type of change are made more frequently as a result of a religious experience, for example con-
version or mystical experience, rather than a result of education.
Growth occurs without education but the process of education
may affect the direction of that growth.

'Development' is frequently used in relation to 'staff development' or 'professional development': it is clearly a form of growth.
The direction of the growth, however, needs clarification. Staff
development might mean that management hopes that, as a result
of some education or training, staff will fit into the company's
mould a little better, so that the square peg actually becomes a
little more rounded. If this is the aim of staff development, then
education which liberates people to be critically aware of the
factors that affect their professional practice may not be the
form of learning that the company desires. Training, on the
other hand, may be a more significant mode of achieving such
ends. By contrast, the company may be seeking to develop professional practitioners who are critically and professionally aware,
so that continuing education may be a means to this end.

Even so, there is much more to professional development than
this since knowledge is not static and new research findings may
call for reconsideration of either theory or practice. However
professional the practitioner, it is often beneficial for him to be
able to spend time away from the practice considering carefully,
in the company of fellow-professionals, the usefulness of new
knowledge and its implications for practice. Additionally, technological innovations are also occurring with greater rapidity,
so that practitioners using these may require time to familiarise
themselves with new equipment.

Professional development and personal growth have been
discussed here as being separate phenomena but Taylor (1980:
336-8) has claimed that, in the field of school teacher education,
professional development and personal growth may occur simul-
taneously because in-service education is not simply a matter
of conferences and courses but a participative activity in the

design of the process. Taylor is right to claim that continuing
education should result in personal growth as well as professional
development, in as much as all education has a humanistic basis
and is, therefore, concerned with the participants. Yet it must
be recognised that while both personal and professional development may occur in continuing education, they are not necessarily
identical nor would it be wise to treat them as synonymous terms.

To what extent should a profession force its members to be
involved in continuing education? School teachers are free to
opt out of attending in-service courses, whereas midwives have
to attend a refresher course every five years. It might be argued
that the person who maintains his professional ideology during
practice and has managed to keep abreast with reading about
new developments in his field does not necessarily need to be
compelled to attend in-service education. True, but he may wish
to do so in order to meet fellow practitioners and discuss new
innovations with them. But not all practitioners retain their
professional ideology, not all keep abreast with changes and
developments, so the laggards need to be forced to keep abreast.
Since it is not possible to evaluate the work performance of
every practitioner and because many who do keep abreast would
not object to undertaking continuing education, it may be
beneficial to both clients and practitioners to enforce the ruling
that every practitioner should attend regular courses. Yet, is
this not contrary to the freedom of the professional? But freedom without responsibility is a form of libertarianism that may
result in unprofessional practice. Therefore, it is incumbent
upon the profession to ensure that its members are responsible
practitioners, so that it might be argued that it should enforce
attendance at these courses. Yet no firm evidence may be cited
to demonstrate that such courses result in a better standard of
professional practice. Indeed, impact evaluation (Le Breton et
al. 1979) of continuing education remains in its infancy in the
United Kingdom. Since research in this field needs to be undertaken, it appears that insufficient evidence exists to persuade
a profession to enforce its practitioners to attend continuing
education. If positive evidence did exist, then the profession
may not need to insist that its members regularly attend in-
service courses because professionals would seek to do so of
their own accord.

TOWARDS A JUSTIFICATION OF THE EDUCATION
OF PROFESSIONALS

'Education, in its broadest sense, is the means of . . . social
continuity of life' (Dewey 1916: 2). Dewey argues that in order
for society to survive it is necessary to transmit the aims and
habits of a social group from one generation to another. Clearly
much of this transmission occurs in the socialisation of the
young, but the process is formalised in initial education, when

the educators select and transmit facets of culture from one
generation to the next. In a similar manner it is possible to
justify the education of professionals. Each profession develops
its own culture - knowledge, skills, attitudes, values, ethics,
etc. - and thus it must transmit these if there is to be some
continuity of its existence. Hence, the curriculum of basic professional education is a 'selection from the culture' (Lawton 1973:
21) of the profession and the new entrants to the profession
acquire some of this selection during their education, which
they usually have to demonstrate during the examinations.
Therefore, it is possible to justify professional education on the
grounds that, for so long as the profession itself has a role in
the society, it is necessary for it to survive by recruiting new
entrants who have to learn its culture. Hence, professional
education may be justified in terms of one of its functions - that
it is the means by which the profession prepares new recruits
to enter its ranks, thereby ensuring the continuity of the
profession.

Yet it might be claimed here that if this were the justification
for professional education, it is making its existence dependent
upon the existence of the profession. It is self-evident that this
particular form of education is dependent upon the existence of
a specific profession. However, this claim might fall into the
trap of utilitarianism. But education must actually have an end-
product, so that it is hardly surprising that professional
education does discover some of its rationale for existence in the
existence of the profession itself. But the profession is not the
end-product of professional education, the recruits to the profession and the practice that they undertake as a result of their
education are its end-products.

Hence it may be argued that those who undertake the educational process are both part of the process and its product.
They, the learners, are the main reason for its existence, for
without learners there can be no educational process and the
educational institution's existence cannot be justified. In this
sense Dewey (1916: 50) was correct when he argued that 'the
educational process has no end beyond itself, it is its own end'.

Aiding those who learn to grow and develop as human beings,
so that they may offer a service to others, is sufficient reason
for the existence of professional education.

THE VALUE OF THE HUMAN BEING

It has been suggested consistently that values are placed upon
phenomena by people. That value is not in the object, nor in a
piece of academic work produced by learners, nor in a phenomenon but it is attributed by those who have in some way or
another had experience of it. Taken to its logical extreme, it
might be possible to argue that, therefore, the human being
himself, life itself, has no intrinsic value but only the value that

others place upon him and his life. Therefore, all values are relative and reflect only the power that enforces their acceptance, so that dominant values are only the values of those who are in social control. This might be true sociologically. For instance, in many societies the life of the low born or slave was not valued as highly as the life of the priest or the monarch. Hence, manifest values in a society are often the values of the elite. Even so, the slave and his life are still valuable to him and to his loved ones. This is true for all people whatever their position in society. Thus it is argued here that the logical outcome is that the human being and life itself are intrinsically valuable. Hence, it is only logical to claim that all phenomena or experiences that enrich life are valuable and those that threaten it are malevolent and to be shunned.

It is for this reason that it may be claimed that education is a worthwhile enterprise, not because it is valuable in itself but because it may enrich the life of those who participate in it.

CONCLUSION

Many themes have been covered in this book, some in a rather cursory manner. Few answers have been provided but rather the process of the education of professionals has been viewed from a humanistic and idealistic perspective. It is hoped that those who are employed in this branch of education may have been encouraged to explore, or to re-examine, some of these central issues so that the body of knowledge about the education of professionals may be expanded and incorporated into the wider literature on the education of adults.

BIBLIOGRAPHY

ACACE (1979) 'Towards Continuing Education', Advisory Council
for Adult and Continuing Education, Leicester.

Alford, H.J. (ed.) (1980) 'Power and Conflict in Continuing
Education', Wadsworth Publishing Co., Belmont.

Allport, G.W. (1954) The Historical Background of Modern Social
Psychology in Lindzey, (ed.).

Apps, J.W. (1979) 'Problems in Continuing Education', McGraw-
Hill Book Co., New York.

Ayer, A.J. (1956) 'The Problem of Knowledge', Penguin,
Harmondsworth.

Bantock, G.H. (1952) 'Freedom and Authority', Faber and Faber
Ltd, London.

Belbin, E. and Belbin, R.M. (1972) 'Problems in Adult Retraining',
Heinemann, London.

Berg, I. (1973) 'Education and Jobs', Penguin, Harmonsworth.

Berger, P.L. and Luckmann, T. (1967) 'The Social Construction
of Reality' Allen Lane/The Penguin Press, London.

Beswick, F.B. (1976) The Education of the Doctor in Turner and
Rushton (eds.).

Bligh, D.A. (1971) 'What's the Use of Lectures', D.A. and B.
Bligh, Briar House, Exeter.

Bloom, B. (ed.) (1956) 'Taxonomy of Educational Objectives
Book I. The Cognitive Domain', Longman, London.

Boley, B.A. (ed.) (1977) 'Crossfire in Professional Education',
Pergamon Press Inc., New York.

Bradshaw, J. (1977) The Concept of Social Need in Fitzgerald
et al. (eds.).

Bucher, R. and Strauss, A. (1961) Professions in Progress,
'American Journal of Sociology' (January).

Caplow, T. (1954) 'The Sociology of Work', University of
Minnesota Press, Minneapolis.

Carlsberg, B.V. (1976) The Education of the Accountant in
Turner and Rushton (eds.).

Carr-Saunders, A.M. (1928) 'The Professions: Their Organization
and Place in Society', Clarenden Press, Oxford.

Cogan, M.L. (1953) Toward a Definition of Profession, 'Harvard
Educational Review', vol. 23, Winter.

Crittenden, B. (1972) Teaching, Educating and Indoctrinating
in Snook (ed.).

Dave, R.H. (ed.) (1976) 'Foundations of Lifelong Education',
Pergamon Press, Oxford.

Davies, I.K. (1971) 'The Management of Learning', McGraw-

Hill Book Co., London.
— (1976) 'Objectives in Curriculum Design', McGraw-Hill Book Co., London.
Dennis, D. (1980) Graduates: Educated but not Prepared in Evans (ed.).
Dewey, J. (1961) 'Education and Democracy', The Free Press, New York.
Doyle, J.F, (ed.) (1973) 'Educational Judgements', Routledge and Kegan Paul, London.
Durkheim E. (1933) 'The Division of Labour in Society' (trans. G. Simpson), The Free Press, New York.
— (1956) 'Education and Sociology' (trans. S.D. Fox), The Free Press, New York.
Elliott, P. (1972) 'The Sociology of the Professions', MacMillan, London.
Etzioni, A. (ed.) (1967) 'The Semi-Professions and their Organization', The Free Press, New York.
Evans, N. (ed.), (1980) 'Education Beyond School', Grant McIntyre, London.
Faure, E. (Chairman) (1972) 'Learning to Be', UNESCO and George Harrap, London.
Finniston, M. (1980) Lifelong Learning for the Professions in Evans (ed.).
Fitzgerald, M. Halmos, P., Murcie, J. and Zoldin, D. (eds.) 'Welfare in Action', Routledge and Kegan Paul in association with the Open University, London.
Frankena, W.K. (1973) The Concept of Education Today in Doyle (ed.).
Freidson, E. (1970) 'Professional Dominance', Atherton Press Inc., New York.
Freire, P. (1972) 'Pedagogy and the Oppressed' (trans. M.B. Ramos), Penguin, Harmondsworth.
Gagné R.M. (1977) 'The Conditions of Learning' 3rd Edition. Holt, Rinehart and Winston, New York.
Gibson, S.J. and Jarvis, P. (1982) The Format and Procedure of the Written Examination in District Nursing, 'Nursing Times' January.
Goode, W.E. (1957) Community within a Community: the Professions, 'American Sociological Review', vol. 25, August.
— (1973) 'Explorations in Social Theory', Oxford University Press, New York.
Greenwood. E, (1957) The Attributes of a Profession, 'Social Work', vol. 2, no. 3.
Griffin. C, (1978) 'Recurrent and Continuing Education', Association of Recurrent Education, Nottingham University.
Gross, R. (1977) 'The Lifelong Learner', Touchstone Books, New York.
Hall, R.H. (1969) 'Occupations and the Social Structure', Prentice Hall Inc., New Jersey.
Halmos, P. (1978) The Concept of Social Problem 'Open University DE206 Course Unit 1', Milton Keynes.

Hamilton, D. (1976) 'Curriculum Evaluation', Open Books, London.

Hare, R.H. (1964) Adolescents into Adults in Hollins (ed.).

Hartog, P. and Rhodes, E.C. (1935) 'An Examination of Examinations', MacMillan, London.

Hartog, P. and Rhodes, E.C. (1836) 'The Marks of Examiners', MacMillan, London.

Hegarty, T.B. (1976) Education for the Legal Professions in Turner and Rushton (eds.).

Hickson, D.J. and Thomas M.W. (1969) Professionalization in Britain - a Preliminary Measurement, 'Sociology', vol. 3, no. 1.

Hiemstra, R. (1975) 'The Older Adult and Learning' University of Nebraska, Lincoln.

Hirst, P.H. (1974) 'Knowledge and the Curriculum', Routledge and Kegan Paul, London.

Hirst, P.H. and Peters, R.S. (1970) 'The Logic of Education', Routledge and Kegan Paul, London.

Hollins, T.H.B. (ed.) (1964) 'Aims in Education', Manchester University Press, Manchester.

Holloman, J.H. (1977) Report of a Conference on Professional Education in Boley (ed.).

Houghton, V. (1974) Recurrent Education in Houghton and Richardson (eds.).

Houghton, V. and Richardson, K. (eds.), (1974) 'Recurrent Education', Ward Lock, London.

Houle, C.O. (1980) 'Continuing learning in the Professions', Jossey Bass Publishers, San Francisco.

Howe, M.J.A. (ed.) (1977) 'Adult Learning', John Wiley and Sons, Chichester.

Hoyle E. and Megarry, J. (eds.) (1980) 'Professional Development of Teachers', World Yearbook of Education, Kogan Page Ltd, London.

Hudson, L. (1966) Selection and the Problem of Conformity in Meade and Parkes (eds.).

Hughes, E. (1958) 'Men and their Work', The Free Press, Glencoe.

— (1963) Professions, 'Daedalus', vol. 92, Fall.

Illich, I. and Verne, E. (1976) 'Imprisoned in a Global Classroom', Writers & Readers Publishing Co., London.

Illich, I. et al. (1977) 'Disabling Professions', Marion Boyars, London.

Irvine, E. (1978) Professional Claims and the Professional Task, 'Open University DE206 Course Unit 27', Open University, Milton Keynes.

Jackson, J.A. (ed.) (1970) 'Professions and Professionalization', Cambridge University Press, Cambridge.

Jarvis, P. (1975) The Parish Ministry as a Semi-Profession, 'Expository Times', vol. LXXXVI, no. 9.

Jarvis, P. and Gibson, S.J. (1980) 'The Evaluation and Training of District Nurse SRN/RGN: the Evaluation of the Implementation of the 1976 Curriculum in Surrey', University of Surrey,

Department of Adult Education.
— (1981) An Investigation into the Validity of specifying 5 'O'
Levels in the General Certificate of Education as an Entry
Requirement for the Education and Training of District
Nurses, 'Journal of Advanced Nursing Studies', vol. 6.
Johnson, T.J. (1972) 'Professions and Power', MacMillan,
London.
Jones, W. (1981) Self Directed Learning and Student Selected
Goals in Nurse Education, 'Journal of Advanced Nursing
Studies', vol. 6.
Kidd, J.R. (1973) 'How Adults Learn', Association Press,
Chicago.
Knowles, M. (1978) 'The Adult Learner: Neglected Species',
2nd edn, Gulf Publishing Co., Houston.
— (1980) 'The Modern Practice of Adult Education', 2nd edn,
Association Press, Chicago.
Knudson, R.S. (1980) An Alternative Approach to the
Andragogy/Pedagogy Issue, 'Lifelong Learning' (April).
Krathwohl, D.R. et al. (eds.) (1964) 'Taxonomy of Educational
Objectives: Book 2 Affective Domain', Longman, London.
Kreitlow, B.W. et al. (1981) 'Examining Controversies in Adult
Education', Jossey Bass Publishers, San Francisco.
Kretch D. and Crutchfield, R.S. (1948) 'Theory and Problems
of Social Psychology', McGraw-Hill Book Co., New York.
Lawson, K.H. (1975) 'Philosophical Concepts and Values in
Adult Education', University of Nottingham, Department of
Adult Education.
— (1982) Concept or Lifelong Education: Policy, 'The
International Journal of Lifelong Education', vol. 1, no. 2.
Lawton, D. (1973) 'Social Change, Educational Theory and
Curriculum Planning', Hodder and Stoughton, London.
Le Breton, P. et al. (eds.) (1979) 'The Evaluation of Continuing
Education for Professionals', University of Washington, Seattle.
Leggatt, T. (1970) Teaching as a Profession in Jackson (ed.).
Lester-Smith, W.O. (1966) 'Education - an Introductory Survey',
Penguin, Harmondsworth.
Lindzey, G. (ed.) (1954) 'Handbook of Social Psychology',
Addison Wesley, Reading, Mass.
Lovell, R.B. (1980) 'Adult Learning', Croom Helm, London.
McGregor, D. (1960) 'The Human Side of Enterprise', McGraw-
Hill Book Co. New York.
MacIntyre, A. (1964) Against Utilitarianism in Hollins (ed.).
Mannheim, K. and Stewart, W.A.C. (1962) 'An Introduction to
the Sociology of Education', Routledge and Kegan Paul, London.
Maslow, A. (1954) 'Motivation and Personality', Harper, New
York.
Meade J.E. and Parkes, A.S. (eds.) (1966) 'Genetic and Environ-
mental Factors in Human Ability', Oliver and Boyd, Edinburgh.
Mehrens, W.A. and Lehmann, I.J. (1978) 'Measurement and
Evaluation in Education and Psychology', 2nd ed., Holt, Rine-
hart and Winston, New York.

Merton, R.K. (1968) 'Social Theory and Social Structure', The Free Press, New York.

Miller, G.A. (1967) Professionals in Bureaucracy: Alienation among Industrial Scientists and Engineers, 'American Sociological Review', vol. 32, no. 5.

Millerson, G. (1964) 'The Qualifying Association - A Study of Professionalization', Routledge and Kegan Paul, London.

Morton, A.J. (1976) Education for the Engineering Profession in Turner and Rushton (eds.).

Musgrave, P.W. (1967) Towards a Sociological Theory of Occupational Choice, 'Sociological Review', vol. 15, no. 1.

OECD (1973) 'Recurrent Education: A Strategy of Lifelong Learning', Organization for Economic Cooperation and Development, Paris.

Open University (1976) 'Report of the Committee on Continuing Education', Open University Press, Milton Keynes.

Parsons, T. (1971) 'The System of Modern Societies', Prentice-Hall Inc., Englewood Cliffs, N.J.

Patterson, R.W.K. (1979) 'Values, Education and the Adult', Routledge and Kegan Paul, London.

Pellegrino, E.D. (1977) Report on a Conference on Professional Education in Boley (ed.).

Peters, R.S. (1966) 'Ethics and Education', George Allen and Unwin Ltd, London.

— (1967) 'The Concept of Education', Routledge and Kegan Paul, London.

Popper, K.R. (1972) 'Objective Knowledge - an Evolutionary Approach', Clarendon Press, Oxford.

Reiss, A.J. (1955) 'Occupations and Social Status', The Free Press, Glencoe.

Rogers, A. (eds.) (1976) 'The Spirit and the Form', University of Nottingham, Department of Adult Education.

Rogers, C.R. (1969) 'Freedom to Learn', Charles E. Merrill, Publishing Co., Columbia, Ohio.

Rogers, E.M. (1962) 'Diffusion of Innovations', The Free Press, Glencoe.

Rowntree, D. (1977) 'Assessing Students - How Shall We Know Them?', Harper and Row Ltd, London.

Ryle, G. (1949) 'The Concept of the Mind', Hutchinson House, London.

Schumacher, E.F. (1977) Good Work in Vermilye (ed.).

Scheffler, I. (1965) 'Conditions of Knowledge', University of Chicago Press, Chicago.

— (1973) 'Reason and Teaching', Routledge and Kegan Paul, London.

Scheler, M. 'Die Wissensfarmen und die Gesellschaft' cited in Merton.

Seebolm, F. (Chairman) (1968) 'Personal Social Services', HMSO, London.

Smith, G. (1978) The Social Work Agency, 'Open University DE206 Course Unit 5', Open University Milton Keynes.

Smith, H. (1977) Adult Learning and Industrial Training in Howe (ed.).

Snook, I.A. (ed.) (1972) 'Concepts of Indoctrination', Routledge and Kegan Paul, London.

Taylor, G.W. Price, P.B., Richards, J.H. and Jacobsen, T.L. (1965) An Investigation of the Criterion Problem for a Group of Medical General Practitioners, 'Journal of Applied Psychology', vol. 49, no. 6.

Taylor, W. (1980) Professional Development and Personal Development in Hoyle and Megarry (eds.).

Tough, A. (1971) 'The Adult's Learning Projects', Institute for Studies in Education, Toronto, Ontario.

Turner, J.R. and Rushton, J. (eds.) (1976) 'Education for the Professions', Manchester University Press, Manchester.

Vermilye, D.W. (ed.) (1977) 'Relating Work and Education', Jossey Bass Publishers, San Francisco.

Ver Steeg, C.L. (1977) Report of a Conference on Professional Education in Boley (ed.).

Vollmer, H.M. and Mills, D.L. (eds.) (1966) 'Professionalization', Prentice-Hall Inc., Englewood Cliffs, NJ.

Weber, M. (1947) 'The Theory of Social and Economic Organizations (trans. A.M. Henderson and T. Parsons), The Free Press, New York.

Wilensky, H.A.L. (1964) The Professionalization of Everyone?, 'American Journal of Sociology', vol. LXX, no. 2.

Williams, B.V. and Huntley J.A. (1979) The Role of the Professional Association in Continuing Education in Le Breton et al. (eds.).

Wilson, B.R. (1965) The Paul Report Examined, 'Theology', vol. LXVlll, no. 536.

Wiltshire, H. (1973) The Concepts of Learning and Need in Adult Education, 'Studies in Adult Education', vol. 5, no. 1, reprinted in Rogers (ed.).

— (1976) The Nature and Uses of Adult Education in Rogers (ed.).

Young, M.F.D. (1971) 'Knowledge and Control', Collier MacMillan Ltd, London.